SU~~~
MAHA~~~

THE TRAVEL GODS MUST BE CRAZY

WACKY ENCOUNTERS IN EXOTIC LANDS

PENGUIN BOOKS

An imprint of Penguin Random House

PENGUIN BOOKS

USA | Canada | UK | Ireland | Australia
New Zealand | India | South Africa | China

Penguin Books is part of the Penguin Random House group of companies
whose addresses can be found at global.penguinrandomhouse.com

Published by Penguin Random House India Pvt. Ltd
7th Floor, Infinity Tower C, DLF Cyber City,
Gurgaon 122 002, Haryana, India

First published in Penguin Books by Penguin Random House India 2019

ISBN 9780143446545

Typeset in Adobe Caslon Pro by Manipal Digital Systems, Manipal
Printed at Thomson Press India Ltd, New Delhi

www.penguin.co.in

For Kapilan, my unrelenting (tor)mentor

Contents

Introduction
All That Glitters in Travel Spiel

Putting one's foot into one's mouth might seem like an impossible feat of contortion requiring complex manoeuvring skills. How and when I acquired and honed these enviable skills is of less interest than the fact that I have managed to deploy them time and time again, during my peregrinations through sixty-five countries in the past quarter of a century. And the consequences have ranged from the embarrassing to the confounding, the costly to the inconvenient, and occasionally, to the downright dangerous.

But how did I turn into that unwonted specimen—a middle-aged, middle-class mother of two from a conservative Tambrahm background travelling solo, long before solo travel became fashionable among Indian women?

It all started with my dear husband (now, of forty years) refusing to foray out of his comfort zone—home and office—whatever the seductions of the beyond, whereas I happened to have just the opposite inclination. On those rare work trips abroad on which I accompanied him, he would invariably assign a local chaperone to show me around all the touristy places. I felt hopelessly shackled and unjustly denied. Soon I developed an irrational disdain for planned trips. From the gloomy depths of a quotidian existence, I secretly longed for the thrills of impromptu forays, the imagined surprises of unpredictability, the pleasures of recklessness. I developed a persistent itch to explore the exciting, exquisite and extraordinary world, which in my sights, was waiting out there. The itch would soon scale up to a full-blown eczema. It could no longer be left untreated.

That was more than two decades ago. I set about looking for 'legitimate' reasons to venture out of my 'discomfort' zone. I ditched my stable but boring job in mainstream print journalism to foray into terra incognita, one that would, hopefully, open the doors to my imagined world of wonder.

Serendipity led me in the direction of energy research, a sari-clad woman bumbling her way through seminar rooms full of smart pinstripes and black ties, poring over zigzagging charts and incomprehensible bar diagrams of NYMEX and Brent. My lexicon was filling up with mumbo jumbo—API index, sour crude, crackers, etc. Before I knew it, I was processing from one conference to the next, having morphed rather quickly into an energy expert.

Soon, invitations began to pour in not just from Kochi or Kolkata, but also from organizers of road rallies and transnational motoring expeditions through petroleum-laden lands—Iran and Azerbaijan where gas wells are still worshipped in fire temples, through the Siberian wastelands where oil gurgles just beneath the ice, through Central Asian steppes once roamed by Genghis Khan's golden horde, now criss-crossed by a welter of metal tubes. Driving in a motorcade of twenty cars ferrying four nationalities through four countries, I was shown wondrous pipelines through which ingenious Chinese engineers had coaxed Burmese oil and gas all the way from Sittwe to distant Yunnan.

My perceived expertise on energy matters even bestowed on me the membership of the prestigious National Security Advisory Board, ostensibly to advise the Indian prime minister on energy-related issues. I also became full-time regulator of India's petroleum industry. I was now on a hurtling gravy train that dropped me off at exotic destinations with dependable frequency. There was a year when I was invited to—hold your breath—eighteen international conferences.

Being always in a hurry—there were PowerPoint presentations to be prepared, leave to be secured, family arrangements to be overseen—I had little time left to do serious homework on the destinations I was headed to. Dog-eared Lonely Planet guides of yesteryears were my only beacons, often blinking or blanking out altogether,

with outdated information on shut-down pensions or
eateries. Eventually, the Internet came along, promising a
modicum of assurance, but its reliability levels were as yet
untested. Which is why I landed up in the Czech Republic
without a valid visa and was caught without yellow fever
vaccination at Nairobi airport.

It never occurred to me to simply go on holidays
depicted on glossy brochures—to leisurely bask in the
sun on golden beaches or sip pina coladas under picnic
umbrellas. Virtually always on a shoestring budget,
rushed for time, and with the destination determined by
conference invites, my trips are eclectic and eccentric.
With my penchant for the uncharted and unexplored, I
even slid off the map whenever I could, and, more than
once, slid off a plane to add some excitement when the
terrain got too barren or dived into the ocean when the
coast seemed predictable. Occasionally, I blundered into
dangerous locations—and had a close escape with my life
or freedom and, on occasion, my dignity.

But, over time, my passion for travel has only gotten
worse. It continues to singe and sear and is now imbued
with a sense of urgency. Not only is there so much to see
and do when I am not getting any younger, the hydra-
headed monster called tourism is literally carpet-bombing
every square inch of our cowering planet—threatening to
reduce me to being a tourist rather than a traveller.

Predictably, friends who insisted on tagging along
with me on my journeys often shunned me like the

plague afterwards. The boat journey up the Mekong River through four countries entailed considerable hardship and yielded no bragging rights, so to speak. As four of us friends sweated it out through sultry, smelly, crowded Vietnamese or Laotian villages and towns, decades-long friendships frayed and fell apart. The trek through the unforgiving jungles of Indonesian Borneo, ostensibly in search of the elusive orangutan, alienated my travel buddies forever thanks to the horrors it entailed.

My friend L, whom I had dragged along to the Galápagos Islands, almost got us detained with her impromptu interview of the then Ecuadorian president, no less, during our chance encounter with him at Quito airport. On another occasion, we nearly got incarcerated in Jordan because my then teenage son had innocuously pocketed an empty cartridge. He has refused to travel with me since. RB, my friend for decades, not just shut me out of her life, but went on to systematically demolish any shred of respectability I might have had, by narrating to all and sundry our undignified quest for a hotel room in the Moroccan city of Fez where she caught me on camera, shinnying up a grimy wall like a lizard.

The last two decades of unplanned travel have taught me one thing. The yonder one dreams about is seldom as glamorous as it is made out to be. The traveller's is a tough life calling for grit and an ability to keep one's cool in the most trying of circumstances. Add to those one's own bunglings, bloomers and botch-ups in unfamiliar landscapes, and you get journeys that become unforgettable for the wrong reasons. But if you retain your sense of humour, it can be fun too, at least in retrospect.

While my indulgent former employer, the well-regarded *Frontline* magazine, faithfully published my lengthy and photo-studded travelogues on strange, unheard-of locations, this book is a rare compilation of candid confessions and unedited impressions that never made it to the page. Other publications like *The Hindu*, *Indian Express*, *Tribune*, etc., too indulged me occasionally and parts of these also find their way into this book. This book would not have materialized without the help and support of Vijay Lokapally, my friend and former colleague, and the unstinting engagement and encouragement of my editor Richa Burman at Penguin Random House India.

At the end of the day, I feel I am incredibly richer for the mosaic of experiences that travel has brought my way, even if they were of the weird and wacky kind. More than the fantasy landscapes I have zipped through and the fancy sights I have feasted my eyes upon, my life has been spiced up by the fascinating assortment of people I have met along the way and the farcical situations I have had to rescue myself from. In these pages, I offer the reader a flavour of what my travels have stirred up.

2017

The ABC of Trekking at Sixty Plus

First, it was Suman, our travel agent in Kathmandu. When we were discussing travel plans on a phone call, and I told him we wanted three porters, one for each of us, he pierced my ego with a patronizing 'Oh you're tourists, not trekkers'. We were headed to Annapurna Base Camp (ABC) in Nepal—P, S and I. ABC is a good two-week trek for the fit and able-bodied, even tougher than the popular Everest Base Camp trek. We were not fit, nor were we seasoned trekkers. I did not bother to explain to Suman that it helps to have both hands available for trekking poles when all three of us are on the wrong side of sixty. From the sarcasm in his tone, I suspected he must be half our individual age.

Next, it was unseen J sitting in distant California. He is the husband of my classmate S with whom my friendship goes back at least half a century. Somehow, J and I had never met. For him, I was an apparition from her previous life, embarking on some foolhardy venture before arthritis claimed me. Our frequent Skype conversations, which he might have overheard, did give him an inkling that something was afoot. But he was certain his sober wife of forty-five years would not be foolish enough to entertain any thoughts of joining her kooky friend on her flights of fancy. In his eyes, S, a responsible mother and a doting grandmother to boot, was incapable of doing something so foolhardy and outrageous. The sheer audacity of our project had lulled him into thinking we were not serious.

Long after we had finalized the itinerary, paid the travel agent and squandered the rest of our hard-earned money on trekking gear and started gymming (me) and hiking (she) regularly, it dawned on J that we meant business. What an outlandish project! No, this can't be allowed to go any further. He whipped up his iPad, consulted Google maps, factored in our daily trekking itinerary, crunched some numbers and voila, came up with the 'exact' number of feet (also metres in parentheses) we would be climbing up each day of the proposed trek. In a six-page detailed analysis of our proposed route, accompanied by an Excel spreadsheet, he showed us how it ranged from a net ascent of 5280.80 feet (1610 metres) on Day Two to 4231.2 feet (1290 metres) on Day Ten, with wide variations in-between. The calculations also showed a maximum net descent of −8888.8 feet (−2710 metres) on Day Twenty-three. Bungee-jumping into the Grand Canyon must seem easier in comparison. No, surely S won't be able to handle this—what if she had a fall and broke her leg or got crippled with a severe back injury? Being a scientist, he waved his impressive spreadsheet before his wife, in the hope of dissuading her. She, in turn, waved it at me on Skype. I cut her off promptly, blaming it on poor digital connectivity in India.

Lo, the imperial capital of Mustang province, nestles in a depression among the towering ranges of Dhaulagiri and Annapurna

What J didn't know, and we would find out the hard way, was that even Google Maps cannot accurately measure the exact ups and downs on the trek. J was spot on in computing the net ascent and descent on a single day, but he completely missed the myriad ups and downs within this undulating terrain where you go up a little and again down, and then up—repeatedly. J was surely way off the mark—it was much worse than he had predicted. But what he did predict seemed dire enough—he believed—for us to drop a project that, according to him, was not just crazy or dangerous, but also unwarranted. Little did he realize this was our swansong, our last-ditch effort to cling on to our imagined mastery over our bodies to do our bidding, our burning desire to do something that would give us bragging rights for the rest of our lives.

S's husband, and my own long-suffering spouse wisely refrained from prying into the finer details of our itinerary, having long given up on efforts to put sense into us. Mali just mumbled something about how I'd rue my decision and probably turn back halfway.

Friends and family too weighed in with their unlimited advice and limited appreciation of our tenacity. I was alternately bullied, cajoled, condescended to. Someone even suggested he would teach me how to Photoshop my picture against the backdrop of the Annapurna range to get likes on Facebook! Meanwhile, a shopkeeper in California managed to scare S into buying a few expensive roundels of self-heating pads to be strapped to the stomach should temperatures on the trail plummet below zero. Her alarmed daughters, for their part, had loaded her luggage with toe gels and other fancy trekking stuff which would be the envy of Chris Bonington but utterly useless on this trek. They just added to our luggage and our poor porters ended up lugging these up and down.

Dinesh, our guide on the trek, was somewhat taken aback when he first set eyes on the three of us at Kathmandu airport—three frumpy grannies in outrageous costumes borrowed from their granddaughters. But he was a suave lad, with a degree of sophistication that belied his youthful years. He quietly changed our original itinerary, which had been designed for a seasoned trekker, to one that would suit hobbling women in ill-fitting new shoes and with wheezing lungs. Seeing us painfully puffing our way up on day one, Dinesh would discreetly dispatch one porter ahead to reserve beds for us in the next teahouse so that we did not have to bivouac under a starry sky in leopard

Sand sculpted by vicious winds in Gilling, en route to Lo Manthang

land. We would eventually drag ourselves to the assigned teahouse around teatime.

The porters, all just out of their teens, told us how much we resembled their grandmothers, perhaps hoping to ingratiate themselves to us. We fumed silently and reserved our revenge for tipping day. Mercifully, the fellow trekkers, a motley lot from across the world, chose to ignore us. After all, they too were huffing and puffing up the slopes, too exhausted to notice the wrinkles on our faces. An occasional Indian trekker would solicitously ask, '*Mataji*, are you all right?' He would hold my hand and gently lead me up a particularly difficult stretch, while his companion would grit his teeth and wonder loudly, '*Ghar mein pota poti ke saath* time *bitaane ke bajaaye kyun kasht kar rahi ho?*' Had it been a pilgrimage destination like Kailash Mansarovar or Amarnath, we might have been forgiven for undertaking this trek, but this was ABC with nary a temple worth its name.

But we donned our thickest skins, and plodded on gamely, unpatronized and unpatronizable. After eight days of negotiating very steep and seemingly never-ending jagged and crooked steps, stumbling over scree, rock and slippery snow, we finally reached the base of the mighty Annapurna. Fitter trekkers might have done it in five days, but we were in no hurry.

When we reached our final destination, there were still fifteen minutes to go before sunrise. In the pale glow of dawn, shadowy forms shuffled towards the ridge that was already populated by a dense concentration of heads silhouetted against a greying sky. Annapurna and her magnificent siblings were still clothed in mist. In a few minutes, a shaft of gold pierced through the mist on the east to reveal the crown of Annapurna South. The shaft moved sensuously to caress the peaks one by one—Baraha Shikar, and then, the grandest of them all, Annapurna I— before moving west to its three younger siblings. Soon the shaft became a flood and the whole range was illuminated in a dazzle of molten gold. In the next half hour, it turned to silver. It was breathtaking, figuratively this time. All the huffing and puffing over the previous week became a mere blip in our memory.

Of course, I needed a close-up view of the glacier at the foot of the range. I was scrambling through slippery ice for a vantage point. One of my trekking poles went tumbling down the side on to the frozen slush. I had another week of treacherous rocks to negotiate on the way down. How would I manage without the second pole?

I need not have worried. The ever-resourceful Dinesh managed a branch in this treeless landscape, which he sharpened and shaped into a pole for me to use on my descent. The porters and guides here are pole-free wonders, nimble and fleet-footed, skipping over the rocks and scree that so challenge the rest of us.

If you think we got a rousing welcome when we returned home intact, think again. There was nary a squeak from any of our detractors. My husband just shrugged his shoulders,

Coiffuring is challenging business in windy Jomsom, the starting point for the Mustang trek

secretly hoping we would not be emboldened now to repeat this foolhardy venture to yet another mountain next year, a wish that must have resonated with P's spouse as well. S's American family promptly pre-empted any such possibility by declaring their intention to henceforth take family holidays to Mexico and Latin America instead of wasting their resources and time on nostalgic trips to Asia.

2008

Awed and Outwitted by Egypt's Gifts

You may choose to go to Aswan for your own reasons. You might be an Agatha Christie fan stalking the 'Old Cataract' out of sheer nostalgia, an archaeologist enamoured of real antiquity for a change—in a world full of fake ones, an admirer of Egypt's former president Abdel Nasser for cocking a snook at the British by building the Aswan High Dam. Be advised—you will, in all probability, be lured into deceptively mundane pursuits, despite yourself.

Aswan's placid streets don't seem to be overrun by tourists, even though, as if in anticipation, the town is peppered with 'Papyrus Institutes' and 'perfumeries' waiting to ensnare the unwary traveller. And your guide can be extremely persuasive in leading you to these lairs. Should you be foolish enough to wander into any of these establishments, you would have indeed crossed the point of no return. Even before you realize what's happening, you're shepherded into a garishly designed lobby and surrounded by a posse of shrewd and extremely aggressive salesmen who take vantage positions to block your exit. A lurid red liquid in a stem glass—which you later find out is an unpalatable drink made out of dried hibiscus flower—is thrust into your hands and you are pushed on to cushions and sofas. The manager, dressed like a bouncer at a disco, soon materializes, and with his practised eye, swoops down on the 'boss' of the group—the one who can make purchase decisions and loosen purse strings. In fact, everyone in Egypt, from tonga-wallah to souvenir salesman, seems to have the uncanny knack of accurately identifying the 'boss'.

And then the blitzkrieg begins, on essential oils and lotus and its significance in ancient Egyptian folklore and how it can cure everything from arthritis to asthma—this, looking at your middle-aged midriff bulging ominously, and how it can enhance your vitality and vigour—this, with a meaningful glance at your menfolk. You give in, if only to stop the filibuster sales spiel. Many vials are thrust into your hands and you are shepherded to the cash counter. The walls are lined with photographs of the manager with film stars, sportsmen and celebrities, all grinning nervously like lambs en route to the abattoir. Your wallet is considerably lighter and your heart commensurately heavier as you emerge from this ordeal laden with an assortment of bottles shaped like minarets and domes and all filled probably with coloured water.

The Nile appears even bluer in Aswan and of course it has swelled, like a pregnant woman, to a lovely lake—Lake Nassr—formed by the Aswan High Dam that turned the barren desert into verdant swatches of sugar cane, mango and banana plantations.

The Aswan Dam has an interesting history that is linked to the history of the Suez Canal. The Suez Canal, a narrow channel between the Red Sea and the Mediterranean, built in 1869, was a huge boon to the West, whose oil supplies from the Middle East would otherwise have to take a circuitous route around Africa. Although built by Egypt, largely with forced labour, the canal was controlled by the British and the French who had vested interests in it.

When Nasser wanted to build the Aswan Dam on the Nile to stop the annual flooding and to generate electricity to light up homes in Egypt, he had originally negotiated financial assistance from Britain and the US.

But then came the Cold War era. Nasser's refusal to side with the US against Russia (he was a buddy of Nehru and Tito who spearheaded the Non-Aligned Movement) and his perceived proximity to the latter put paid to the loan agreement. A determined Nasser decided to nationalize the Suez Canal and collect tolls from passing ships to fund the dam. Naturally, this precipitated an international crisis. Britain, France and Israel teamed up to invade Egypt, but were thwarted by the UN and the US. Since then, the Suez has remained with the Egyptians—their pride and their highest source of income.

Understandably, your guide too swells with pride when he narrates the history of the Aswan High Dam. He even tells you that the Statue of Liberty was originally meant for the Suez Canal, but got diverted to the newly independent confederacy of American states.

After Aswan, we're off to Abu Simbel, deep into the Nubian Desert on the Sudanese border. Travellers to Abu Simbel have to move in a convoy that leaves twice a day, once before sunrise and again around 11 a.m. Ever since a bunch of rogue Nubian tribesmen—allegedly Sudanese—swooped on a busload of Canadian and European tourists and stabbed quite a few of them to death some years ago, the Egyptian government takes no chances. In fact, in most parts of Egypt, Tourism Police are ubiquitous, and here, they tote guns and

Carvings in the temple at Abu Simbel

pistols. After all, isn't tourism Egypt's second highest money-spinner after the Suez Canal? But this feels more like being led to a concentration camp in the middle of the desert than to the historical treasure that Abu Simbel is.

The temple at Abu Simbel has its back to the visitor. In order to access it, you have to navigate a minefield of persistent Nubian salesmen chorusing 'Namaste' and hurling in rapid-fire the names of our Bollywood heroes in the hope you'd buy their kitsch. You dodge them deftly and go around a barren mountain and suddenly come upon the three massive statues, each 20 metres high and depicting Ramesses II in a seated position watching over the Nile for any intruders who might be foolhardy enough to challenge his supremacy.

Relief Carvings of Nubian slaves in the temple at Abu Simbel

Carved out of the rocky mountain on the west bank of the Nile, the temples dedicated to gods Ra Harakhty, Amun and Ptah—apart from Ramesses II, ancient Egypt's mightiest and much admired monarch—were an accidental discovery. Swiss explorer Jean-Louis Burckhardt chanced upon just a massive head jutting out of a sand mound. The temple was then excavated and dusted and put on display. When the Aswan Dam was built, the temples were in danger of being submerged by Lake Nasser. A conscientious Egyptian government then had it shifted painstakingly, stone by carved stone, to its present site.

The temple of Hathor II in Abu Simbel

Even as you're gaping at the statues, an alabaster jar is thrust into your hands. It is indeed beautifully translucent and very light. As you're admiring the jar, holding it up against the sun to see the patterns, it crumbles into a million pieces and scatters to the ground. This is what the Bedouin salesman was waiting for. You cough up the extortionate price that he insists you pay. It is only much later you find out that this is a standard con job in these parts and that alabaster is too delicate to even hold.

Few visitors stay on in Abu Simbel, which has just a couple of hotels, both overpriced. But with such excellent roads, whoever would think of staying back? On our way back, I chat with Atta, our guide, and tell him it must be a difficult name to have these days—9/11 had happened just a few years before. Atta is unfazed by this patronizing comment from a boorish Indian woman. 'Oh, because of 9/11? In Egypt, Atta is not only a common surname, but it also means Gift from the Gods.'

2010

Oktoberfest: The Goblet of Bacchus

Avoid Munich in October. It's that time of the year when the city's denizens and visitors lose their collective marbles to hilarious effect. Oktoberfest is an unmitigated (but not altogether unpleasant) assault on all your senses—visual, auditory, tactile, gustatory and olfactory. Of course, everyone present, including you, is both perpetrator and victim. During the fest, Munich in the evenings is a visual delight, with millions of twinkling fairy lights complemented by brightly illuminated rides and roller coasters. One can indulge in every juvenile whim and fancy: get tossed in a swirling merry-go-round that rides up a pole and opens like a giant umbrella to hurl you upside down, drop down in a stomach-churning devil trap through a vertical shaft or saunter through an artificial cave to confront demons and monsters.

To indulge in some real action though, head to one of the many tents put up by Bavaria's famous breweries. The collective chatter of a few thousand voice boxes is loud enough to drown out various bands gamely trying to produce music above the din.

The fest rules require you to be seated, however precariously, to be served beer. That's easier said than done. Each brand has its own hall and there are several of these. Your hall may be as big as a football stadium, with hundreds of benches jammed closely together. But the place is teeming with humanity, all crammed into these benches and many standing on tables trying to catch the attention of passing barmaids. If you want a seat, you will have to push, shove and crash into groups of total strangers who are equally determined to not let you in. It takes much ingenuity, oodles of charm and powerful 'elbow' work to wrest a spot. Once you have accomplished this, half the battle is won.

And then begins part two of your ordeal—catching the eye of the barmaids. You may stand on the benches, bellow, scream, hail, wave and look like a buffoon, but no one minds. Either they are too drunk to care or themselves trying their brand of buffoonery. After several tries, one finally manages to have a barmaid's wavering attention for a split second in which you thrust two crisp €10 notes into her apron pocket. She disappears into the mass of humanity and there is no sign of her for the next half an hour. Not that you need the beer to get into the spirit of the evening;

after all, the tent is so reeking with alcohol that you just need to breathe deeply. Everyone is happily sloshed and most have collapsed on their benches with abandon, their limbs stretched out languorously.

With your fellow benchers in a state of surrender to Bacchus, you eye their drink, wondering if they'd notice if you took a swig. With a furtive glance all around, you reach for one of the many glasses on the table, but a hand promptly comes down like a guillotine to cut you off. Shamefacedly, you try to pretend to be as drunk and manage a weak smile.

Finally, the barmaid heaves into view, her slender wrists balancing six massive glasses in each hand, the frothy golden liquid sloshing all over the place. Also doing the rounds are young women dressed like milkmaids and hawking assorted eats, including pretzels as big as steering wheels.

Earlier in the evening, as I took the metro to the site of the fest, it was filled with men and women in traditional costumes that might have been worn 200 years ago when the first year of the festival was celebrated to commemorate the union of Crown Prince Ludwig to Princess Therese. Girls in golden braids and milkmaid costumes with partners in breeches and funny hats are a common sight. It is as though you're in the Bavaria of yore—if you ignore the setting, that is.

There are posters in the city that tell you how, in the previous year, more than 6 million visitors downed

7 million litres of beer, and munched on several thousand yards of sausages. According to a news report, visitors lost or left behind 'one hearing aid, a leather whip, a live rabbit, a tuba, a ship in a bottle, 1450 items of clothing, 770 identity cards, 420 wallets, 366 keys, 330 bags and 320 pairs of glasses, 90 cameras and 90 items of jewellery and watches. A total of 37 children were also lost'. One can well imagine how much they must have enjoyed themselves to accomplish this feat!

After a drinking spree, if you can still stagger out of the tent, there are hordes of rickshaws waiting outside to take you back to your hotel long after the metro and buses stop running. But make sure you don't stay too close to the fest venue, or you will end up being awake all night, due to continuous wails of ambulance sirens as they ferry drunken revellers to hospitals in the city. But make no mistake, the same drunken revellers will return to the same fest ground the next day to do it all over again. It is that irresistible!

2003

Time Travelling to Issyk-Kul

It seems a minor miracle that we survived the landing, considering the extent of blinding snow all around the tarmac. Our tiny Uzbek Air plane of Soviet provenance was probably held together more by the indomitable will of its engineer than by the laws of physics. As I stumble out of Bishkek airport at this unearthly hour—it is past six in the evening, nearly three hours after sunset in winter in the Kyrgyz capital—there is a single taxi parked at some distance. I dart out, braving the blizzard, skid over the ice to make my way to the rickety Lada. With nary a by-your-leave, I yank open the back door and dive in.

Maximilian Alexandrovich—I would learn his name later—the grizzly Russian driver was obviously not expecting any passengers this evening. He stares at me blankly. From the fumes inside the cab, I presume he is in a vodka-induced daze. I wonder if ex-Soviet taxi drivers consider passengers an occasional interruption to their daily schedule of lazing around in their cabs. I also wonder whether it is wise to hire his taxi, but unfortunately, there is no other outside Bishkek airport tonight.

I had not planned it this way. I was to arrive in Bishkek by noon, take a cab directly to Lake Issyk-Kul six hours away and check into Abror Gastanista, recommended by my good friend R. But my plans went awry when the flight from Tashkent to Bishkek was delayed by six hours. Now I have no hotel bookings, speak no Russian and have to survive by my wits in this strange city.

Optimistically, I show the cab driver the scrap of paper on which R had scrawled the name of my Issyk-Kul hotel in Russian. Maxim mumbles incomprehensibly, groans, turns the paper upside down and holds it inches away from his nose. This is going to take a while. After a volley of more incomprehensible exchange—mine in Tamil and English, his in Russian, a lot of it swear words, I presume—and much gesticulating, it finally dawns on him that I am asking him to take me all the way to Lake Issyk-Kul, not to Hotel Issyk-Kul in Bishkek. Then follows a complex mime act as to how many days I plan to stay there and whether he should also bring me back to Bishkek. Finally, we arrive at the price of $200 for the package. The taxi will stay in Issyk-Kul all three days and bring me back to Bishkek (or at least that's what I hope his understanding is).

He is still grumbling, half talking to himself, shaking his head, gesticulating. I jam a $100 bill into his grimy hands and gesture him to get going. Reluctantly he starts the car. As the heating comes on, tempers cool down. Fitful attempts at conversation prove futile. I draw my jacket around my shoulders and stretch out on the back seat of the Lada. I have enough time to rue my foolishness in not staying back at the airport that night and to pray that he takes me to my desired destination.

Eventually, the car screeches to a halt and I am jolted out of my slumber. It is still dark, although there is a flicker of light somewhere in the distance. We have stopped in front of a locked gate with a winding driveway behind it. But there is no building in sight, nor any signboard. I notice the snow swept neatly off the road on to the sidewalks has turned into ice. There hasn't been any fresh snowfall that night.

Maxim gets out of the car, scales the gate, jumps on to the other side and is off without a word. My stupor is rapidly replaced by rising apprehension. The seconds crawl. At last, I spy two forms shuffling towards the gate. Maxim probably came back in five minutes, but in my disorientated and torporific state, it could well have been hours. The other man has a huge key bunch and a torch. He fiddles with a couple of keys before finding the right one to unlock the gate. Maxim gets back into the car and we drive half a kilometre or so to reach the main entrance of Abror Gastanista, or so I believe, vaguely making out the Cyrillic script.

When I enter the precincts, I feel as if I have stepped through a time machine. The lobby is as cold and still as a crypt. There are life-size wooden chessmen and women placed on the chequered floor at one level. The hall is high-roofed and massive and there is a flaring central staircase with translucent marble steps. The carved banisters are peppered with statues holding up unlit torches. The red carpeting is slightly mouldy. Several over-ornate chandeliers give the lobby a cinematic opulence although the place is devoid of any signs of life.

Maxim leads me to the reception desk where no one seems to be around. But then as we approach the counter, we spot a diminutive babushka dozing off behind a glass case full of matryoshka dolls. We tap the counter and she wakes up with a jolt. She reacts as though she has seen a ghost and I almost return the compliment. She is not expecting any guests in October, the start of winter in the Tien Shan mountains. I did not have a reservation either. R had assured me it was not necessary since the *gastanista* has more than a hundred rooms and unlikely to be fully booked off-season.

If you're wondering why and how I chose to go to remote Issyk-Kul of all places, that too in winter, here goes: ever since I had seen a centre spread picture of the mysterious vast blue expanse fringed by snow peaks in a magazine—probably *National Geographic*—I had come to covet this placid lake in the middle of nowhere. My desire was fuelled not a little by the ecstatic descriptions of my friend R who had visited Issyk-Kul many times during his university days in Tashkent. So, when an opportunity came to travel to Tashkent on work, R urged me to go to Issyk-Kul, never mind the season. Seldom do such opportunities come one's way and one must seize the day, he insisted.

With Maxim doing all the talking, it transpires the babushka is happy to accommodate me for the next three days for a princely sum of $25 a day, all meals included. I pay up and hand over my passport for photocopying. Maxim gestures to indicate he would go and stay somewhere else and would come back at 10 a.m. By now, Maxim and I seem to have evolved a mutually comprehensible sign language. The babushka lifts my bag effortlessly and leads me down the corridor to a heritage elevator with collapsible grill gates. Instead of buttons, the elevator has old-fashioned round switches with numbers painted under each switch. She throws the switch (do you ever wonder what *throwing* a switch means?) for Floor 5, and the elevator takes off with a jolt. It makes so much noise—enough to drown out a jet engine taking off—that I fear it will shatter the glass panes.

On Floor 5, there is a long corridor with rooms on one side, much like a hospital rather than a hotel. Everything is blinding white—the doors, walls, windows, balustrades. I later learn that it is indeed a sanatorium where Soviet big bosses used to holiday in summers. Now it is used by Kyrgyz bosses who bring their mistresses whenever they can. The babushka leads me through several corridors and finally reaches one where she opens a door and signals me in; she then turns back wordlessly and disappears down the long corridor.

I enter the room and survey my surroundings. It seems straight out of a period film from the Soviet era. The decor was so outré it would have made Shahnaz Hussain blush. The bed is a high four-poster with a heavy mattress and brocade sheets on it; one wall is completely glass, curtained by frilly, transparent nylon with lace borders. The enormous bathroom has an enamel washbasin on a white-painted iron stand and a massive bathtub standing on curved lion feet made of metal. The mirror is ornate and so are the lamp fittings. This must be the presidential suite reserved for the commissars in Soviet times.

The overwrought clock on the table tells me it is already 7 a.m. I go up to the windows and part the lace curtains and jump back in amazement. In the dawn glow, the view is simply spectacular. The pink-tinged snow peaks of the majestic Tien Shan range are almost at touching distance. In the foreground, just below the window, is a shimmering lake, with its waters gently lapping against the snowy bank. This is even better than the picture that has haunted me all those years, I tell myself. The snow is fresh and sparkles like diamond. The silence is so deafening I could hear my own heartbeat. I stand mesmerized for a few moments. But I am tired. I clamber on to the bed and collapse in a heap.

After about three hours, I wake up and get ready to go down for breakfast. That's when I realize how foolish

I have been. I had not made a mental note of the way we came in and am truly lost in the labyrinthine corridors and multiple wings, all of which look alike. A sanatorium with 300 rooms and identical corridors can confound even the janitors and bellboys who work there. There is not a soul in sight and no sign of that heritage elevator. After several minutes of wandering here and there, I spot a staircase and decide to go down. But even after I have descended five floors, the lobby is nowhere in sight. I go through several heavily curtained doors and dark alleyways and suddenly find myself in an industrial-size kitchen with gleaming stainless-steel cooking machinery. Nothing seems to be cooking or sizzling anywhere. Finally, I locate a lone woman in uniform and accost her. Of course she speaks no English, but leads me out of this maze into the dining hall.

It seems like a banqueting hall, heavily chandeliered, smothered in satin curtains with nylon ropes and tassels and packed with hundreds of round tables. The sideboard is neatly stacked with glittering vodka and wine glasses in hand-carved crystal. The Soviet bosses surely dined in style. In season, the dance floor must have rung out with the rhythmic steps of hundreds of restless feet. There is a grand piano at one end of the hall and a well for a full orchestra. Tchaikovsky must have provided a backdrop to the impassioned shouts of 'Nzdazarovia!' in better times. Now the hall wears a deserted look, a grander version of Miss Havisham's, minus the cobwebs.

I am led to a corner table on the edge of the dance floor. Today, I seem to be the lone diner in a hall that could seat several hundred. The attendant slaps some *kasha* (buckwheat porridge) on my plate and goes to fetch some tea from a steaming samovar. As I swallow the milkless, sugarless kasha, I hear some voices—in American English. Five persons—four men and a woman—troop past me, eyeing me with interest. They seat themselves at the table next to mine and steal a few glances at me as they bend over their kasha and omelettes.

I am so grateful for human presence in this eerie, spooky sanatorium that I decide to address them directly. After the usual preliminaries, I gather they are from Manas, the American military base not far from here. They are very surprised to see a lone traveller, that too from India, in this godforsaken spot in Central Asia in the middle of nowhere. They can't fathom why a loony Indian woman would choose to travel alone in winter to this isolated place even if it is paradise. They themselves can't wait to get back home. Thankfully, today is their last day in Manas and they are off home to the US in the evening.

After breakfast, I step out of the hotel. The blizzard from the night before has subsided, and the sun is shining in all its glory, turning the vast virgin snow fields into incandescent plains of the purest white. And looking beyond, I see the lake itself, shimmering in the morning sun, its waters the deepest imaginable shade of blue. And beyond that, an endless range of snow-capped peaks, perfectly framing the scene. And off to one corner, our bent little hotel, dwarfed by its surroundings, half covered with snow, the only man-made speck on the most primordial of landscapes. I had truly reached the end of the earth.

2005

Yazd: Gained in Translation

The elderly caretaker picks up my backpack and leads me down the steps into a cavernous basement. As we are about to enter, we hear a loud shout followed by a flying missile which happens to be a rolled-up newspaper. It lands at my feet. 'Get out!' calls out the disembodied voice, but the caretaker takes no notice. He hands me my backpack and gestures me to go in. As I hesitantly move into the dark doorway, a shadowy form emerges from the room, another missile in hand, but stops in its track. 'Oh, are you going to share my room? Where the hell are you from?' she barks as she ambles back to her bed without waiting for my answer. As my eyes get used to the darkness, I discern the outline of a young woman flopped on one of the two beds in this dingy room without a door. I mumble my provenance, but she is already asleep.

I am in Yazd, the desert town in central Iran, 690 km away from Tehran. It is supposed to be the second oldest continuously inhabited city in the world after Jerusalem. (Didn't Damascus claim this title?) I am staying at an old caravanserai called the Silk Road Hotel recommended by *Lonely Planet*. Of course, this was 2003, long before the inn acquired a high-profile and a fancy website. For $8 a day (Iranians prefer the US dollar to the hassle of counting their rials in hundreds of thousands for equivalent amounts), I am to share this door-less, windowless underground cavern with its other occupant who happens to be a Lebanese banker from Chicago. Joyce had thrown away her lucrative job in Citibank to travel the world. She has been travelling overland for three years now, having started in Japan and working her way west.

If Iran in 2003 was still veiled in multiple sanctions and posed a tantalizing mystery to curious travellers, Yazd was like a woman in an iron burqa, with nary a chink in the armour to excite your imagination. Yazd is not the easiest of destinations to access either; I had to brave an overnight train from Tehran—in an all-ladies compartment with hermetically sealed windows. The smell of the assorted meats as the women unwrapped their dinner packets still haunts me, after years.

Yazd is a fascinating desert town stuck in a time warp. Its labyrinthine streets are lined with adobe houses whose earthy hues are relieved every now and then by exquisite turquoise tile panels and ornamental doorways. The intricately carved

wooden doors have double knockers—a slender one for
women visitors and a sturdy one for men. Depending on
the sound from the knocker, the residents of the house
could decide whether the door would be opened by a male
or female. All this, long before the Islamic revolution with
its strict rules of gender segregation came to overwhelm
present-day Iranians. Yet, the knockers here are just a relic.
There are gender-neutral electric call bells alongside.

Before I could proudly cackle and declare how in India
we never practised this kind of gender segregation, Joyce
put me in my place with the most sobering declaration:
of all the countries she had travelled through, India was
where she had faced the worst sexual harassment. She
narrated harrowing tales of how she had been groped and
pinched, probed and propositioned in most places she had
travelled to.

My journey to Yazd was prompted by the desire to
find out how the descendants of Darius and Xerxes and
other eminences of the formidable Persian pantheon
survive in today's Iran. The Farsi community is said to be
30,000 strong, much less than those who fled to western
India where King Jaidev Rana gave them refuge on the
condition that they marry only within their community.
The language spoken by the Zarathusht in Yazd is different
from the Farsi spoken by Muslims in Iran and the language
spoken by Indian Parsis.

Naturally, it is at the Atashkadeh or Fire Temple that
the Zarathusht, as the original Farsis are called, congregate.

I make my way to the temple and join the fifty-odd worshippers seated in a circle around a young priest. He is expounding on something. His speech is fiery, and his gestures expressive. I understand nothing of what he says, but am mesmerized nevertheless. This goes on and on and after what seems an eternity, they all get up and go through a Kusti ritual. *Kusti* is not unlike the sacred thread used by Brahmins in India, but is worn around the waist.

After the ceremony is over, I befriend the priest, who is a banker. He speaks a smattering of English and is happy to take me in his car to other Fire Temples in Yazd. We drive around Yazd and even visit the Tower of Silence where motorcycle-borne youths race up and down the sandy mounds and kick up dust. I have the privilege of being introduced to important members of the community and take their photographs.

The following day sees me trudging towards the ancient and exquisitely proportioned Jāmeh Mosque, built in the fourteenth century by the governor of Yazd in memory of his wife, Bibi Fatema Khatun. The mosque has a hoary legend. In the fourteenth and fifteenth centuries, it was used by young women to ensnare eligible men. All they had to do was to go up to the top of the minaret and take their pick of the men assembled in the courtyard after Friday prayers. Each woman would then throw down her key at her chosen man and wait with bated breath for him to pick it up. He who picked up the key could claim her for a bride. But with a dense crowd of men of assorted ages congregating in the courtyard after Friday prayers, the practice was more like a Russian roulette and mishaps were common and unintended consequences rife.

The legend has piqued my curiosity and I want to go up to the top of the minaret, if only to visualize how a *swayamvara* could have misfired in ancient Yazd. The real reason of course is to get a good view and snapshots of the warrens that make up the old town—there are no high-rises in Yazd. But there is a huge lock on the door of the stairwell leading up to the minaret. I go in search of the caretaker and gesture to him to open the door to the winding stairs. He promptly gestures back 'no' and supplements it with a vigorous nod. A passer-by comes to my rescue and explains to the caretaker my purpose and points to my camera. The caretaker then insists I give a written requisition. I have no idea what he would do with it, but I oblige him with a hastily scribbled request addressed to the imam of the mosque. I am certain the caretaker could not read English, but he seemed content enough to open the door for me.

I bound up the winding steps of the minaret. A balustrade goes around the pencil top, offering a fantastic view of the sprawling old town. I recall another minaret, also in Iran, in the town of Isfahan, where I had to buy a ticket to go up. That's because the Jonban minaret shook and swayed in the wind and thus became a sensation, which the clergy milked by ticketing it to the public. Mercifully, this one is still and offers a bird's-eye view of the earth-hued roofs and dozens of *badgirs*—cooling towers built

over a *qanat* (opening to an underground water channel)—
which offer natural air-conditioning in the desert. These
are unique views that only the minaret can offer. I lose
track of time as I click different angles of Yazd from this
privileged perch.

Brown and burnt, Yazd, the quintessential desert town in Iran

The sun begins to sink into the desert horizon and I
decide to go back. But when I find my way down the
spiral staircase, the heavily carved wooden door is shut
and seems to be padlocked from outside. I start shouting
and pounding on the door hoping someone is still outside.
There is no response. Only a sinister silence. Panic begins
to well up in me. The prospect of spending the night on
the ledge of the minaret under a starry sky may sound

romantic in retrospect, but I was terrified. Besides, it was getting chilly too.

After a few minutes of fruitless banging and shouting, I go back up on to the minaret tower to see if I can spot anyone. It is already dark and no one seems to be about. I muster all my strength and shout, trying multiple languages—Tamil, English, Hindi. '*Kholo! Kholo! Koi hai?*' I wail. Suddenly I get a response, also in Hindi. '*Kya hai? Ruko, ruko!*' I can't believe my ears. Am I hallucinating already? I spot three heads in silhouettes—seem like women in headscarves coming towards the mosque. I direct them to the door of the minaret and rush down the spiral staircase in pitch darkness. When I reach the landing, I hear the sweet sound of the latch being undone and the door being flung open.

As I burst out of the confines of the minaret, there they are, three women, all my compatriots, chatting in Mumbaiya Hindi. I can't believe my luck! These were Parsis from Mumbai on a pilgrimage to Yazd to worship at the Fire Temple. But for them, I might have spent the night under starry skies on top of a minaret in a desert town in the middle of nowhere. Boy, was I thrilled to find these chatty women, interested in shopping for unique Persian artefacts in the gullies of Yazd! I latch on to them the rest of the evening as well as the next day.

Eventually, they left with the rest of the group now heading to Shiraz. As I aimlessly wander the streets, I bump into another erstwhile Mumbaikar now living in

Canada. Fariborz Rahnamoon from Yazd runs a journal for the Parsi diaspora from distant Vancouver. Once a year, he visits Yazd to see his mother. I spend the afternoon visiting his mother's home in the old part of town. Over tea, he narrates the difficulties faced by his community. *Iranzamin*, his journal, is his modest contribution to keeping the Zoroastrian culture alive.

2010

The Barbed Beauty of Israel

Your brush with Israeli officialdom begins at Ben Gurion Airport itself. We had flown Royal Jordanian into Tel Aviv and queued up before the immigration counter along with other nationalities. All Indians on the flight—about twenty of us—are herded into a room to have our passports scrutinized with minute care. The immigration official is unwilling to buy my explanation that my son and I are in Holy Land on a tour of religious history. If we're neither Christian nor Jewish and obviously not Muslim, why would we want to visit religious places here? The fact that we had our visas stamped on separate sheets of paper—a gracious gesture by the Israel embassy in New Delhi, one that would help us gain entry into Syria, Lebanon and fifty-eight other Arab League countries that are wary of the Israeli stamp on your passport—does not seem to help.

'Do you have any friends in Israel?' The official wants us to call my friend on the phone to talk to him, but my phone's battery has run out and there's no way of getting his number just now. Besides, I didn't even need it since he must be waiting outside at the arrival hall to pick us up. But I can't get to the arrival hall until we clear immigration. After about thirty minutes of frustrating wait, I have a brainwave. 'Why don't you Google his name?' I write down my friend's name for the immigration officer. I don't know what the computer threw up, but her demeanour changes, our passports are returned and we are waved off.

Our friend and his lovely Israeli wife drive us directly to Jerusalem, about ninety minutes away, on world-class highways through typically Mediterranean landscape, hot and dry for the most part. But trust Israelis to turn even adversity to their advantage. As our flight was landing, I had noticed that all rooftops were glinting with solar panels to take advantage of a climate others would have just complained about.

Our impression of the Israeli state's obsession with security is strengthened further as we explore the country over the next ten days. The presence of gun-toting youngsters in army fatigues is ubiquitous and quite unnerving, initially. These are members of the elite IDF or Israeli Defence Forces, and you find them in cafes, restaurants, trains, buses, streets, parks—everywhere. In fact, one is surprised to see young girls in uniform advertising their individuality with very fashionable stiletto shoes or jewellery. These youngsters have been issued firearms on conscription to the IDF soon after school; they serve in the army for two years, and they are responsible for their guns during this period. Some of them seem to take this responsibility a tad too seriously, taking their guns even into public toilets! But perhaps it is just as well, for unlike in the US, in this country, you don't hear of random shootings by youngsters having access to firearms.

Jerusalem lives up to our expectations. The walled city is a warren of lanes walking through which is a journey back in time. We saunter through the cobbled lanes of the Arab quarter with its profusion of merchandise. The flagstones you step on are the very same ones on which Jesus might have walked once, or at least so proclaim the inscriptions. Haggling is as much a part of the transaction as purchase, just like in our bazaars. If you're not smart, you could end up paying the equivalent of $20 for a plate of kebabs in a poky wayside eatery.

You go deep inside the Arab quarter and emerge into a clearing in which stands the Church of the Holy Sepulchre where Christ is interred. It is as gorgeous as it is ancient; there are numerous altars dedicated to various denominations, much like our own ancient temples. There is a tomb-sized marble slab—the Stone of Unction—on the spot where Christ is believed to have been crucified and later resurrected. We're there at evensong and are treated to a ceremonial spectacle where black-robed monks of the Greek Orthodox Church stand around the stone reciting hymns in chorus. The bishop offers incense and we're struck by the similarity of all religious rituals, whatever the faith! It is a mesmerizing moment to be in one of the holiest of holy shrines in all of Christendom at official prayer time.

Within just a few hundred yards, in the Jewish quarter, is a site considered to be the holiest of holy for both Jews and Muslims. But first you go through the Jewish bazaar that hawks kosher meat of every kind, its stalls slung about with sausages and piled high with seafood. Gradually, the Islamic fez gives way to Jewish skullcaps and you see more and more men in black long coats, top hats and sidelocks. They are usually the products of Jewish seminaries or *midrashas*, the equivalent of Islamic madrasas where they devote a part of or even their entire lives learning Jewish scriptures.

Even as the Israelis have appropriated the holy places of other religions—Christianity and Islam—within their territory, they are subject to a taste of their own medicine. The holiest of holy Jewish shrine in the State of Israel is encased in a magnificent mosque that bars entry to all but Muslims. The Temple Mount in Jerusalem housed the original Jewish temple built by Solomon. It was destroyed by the Roman siege of Jerusalem and subsequently came under Muslim occupation. The Muslim kings built a most magnificent octagonal mosque, encasing the original rock of the Jewish shrine, towards the end of the seventh century. The Dome of the Rock or the Al Aqsa mosque is said to be the oldest standing Islamic structure in the world.

Muslim quarter in Jerusalem

We follow a steady stream of Jewish devotees through X-ray machines and body-searching cameras into the Wailing Wall complex. The 57-metre-high Western Wall abuts the Al Aqsa mosque and this is as far as devout Jews can get if they want to worship in their most sacred site. There are hundreds of worshippers, little book in hand, reciting prayers, pressing their heads to the Wall, bemoaning and wailing their inability to access the shrine. The Wailing Wall is indeed a microcosm of ethnic diversity. Jews of all nationalities and ethnicities come to worship here. The women's section of the wall is separated from the men's enclosure. The thousands of cracks in the wall worn by butting heads are stuck with little chits of paper recording the entreaties and petitions of the devout to their Maker.

We make our way to the Dome of the Rock on the other side of the wall through another security barricade manned by Israeli soldiers. The golden dome that beckons to you from everywhere in Jerusalem sits on a gorgeous blue ceramic base, graceful in its perfect symmetry. Being in salwar-kameez, I thought I could enter the mosque if I covered my head and walked purposefully. I walk past the guards without glancing at them, but perhaps something in my demeanour alerts them. They stop me and ask for my name and promptly shoo me off the site. We then wander off to the Armenian quarter to check out their quaint squares and homes. We spot a Chabad House in one of the streets and I am reminded of our very own

Chabad House in Mumbai, one of the targets of the 26/11 atrocities.

Ancient town of Acre in Israel

After a couple of days we take a ramshackle *sheruth*, the ubiquitous Arab minibus (in contrast to the swanky Israeli buses), to a border post reinforced with miles of steel and concrete and wrapped in copious quantities of barbed wire. We are shepherded through narrow steel cages that seem to run for miles. If you want to visit Bethlehem on the Palestinian side, you have to make your way through this cage and brave the security booths and reinforcements that would put Guantanamo to shame. While exiting Israel, the security doesn't stop you. Once in Palestinian territory, you take a taxi to the Church of Nativity 6 km away. We spend the day in Palestine, visiting Ramallah and Jericho, besides the Church of Nativity.

We encounter Israeli officialdom once again on the way back to the Israeli border post. The border security personnel are very much there, but we, some fifty of us, tourists as well as locals, are made to wait for a couple of hours in a narrow and dark enclosure leading to the locked and fortified gate with a festoon of electronic surveillance gadgetry. There are a couple of guards even on a rafter above, toting AK-47s and keeping a watchful vigil on the waiting line below. The waiting crowd is getting restive at the whimsical behaviour of the security personnel and there is a lot of heckling and catcalls to the uniformed Israeli guards manning the gate.

Suddenly a voice looms out of the loudspeaker yelling something in a foreign language, presumably Arabic. We don't comprehend and look up in confusion. The others in the queue are gesticulating wildly, asking us to do something. Then the voice switches to English: 'Hey you, take off your cap, I want to see your face.' We look up, but no sign of any human being anywhere. Then we see a CCTV camera above our heads just outside the fortified gate. The voice belongs to Israeli security and she is actually yelling at my eighteen-year-old son, asking him to take off his cap so that she can see his face. But even after he does that, she is not satisfied. 'Where are you from and what is your business?' calls out the disembodied voice. Terrified, I reply meekly. 'We are from India.' She is not satisfied.

She barks again, asking us to hold out the first page of our passports to the CCTV camera. Which we do with alacrity just in case the finger on the trigger of the AK-47 on the rafter above got a bit itchy! And troop out hastily when the gate opens, thoroughly shaken, to mingle and disappear into the crowds on the Israeli side of the fence.

2006

Bagan: Stepping into a Bioscope

The Mandalay–Bagan boat ride on the Irrawaddy is not for the faint-hearted, especially if you're not travelling in a tour group herded by an ultra-efficient guide. You have to survive the trishaw ride to the boat jetty at 4 a.m., jostle for your space in the queue on a very wobbly gangplank, convince the inscrutable Myanmarese officialdom that you're not a spy and, finally, after obtaining that much-sought-after ticket for $16, weave your way through a maze of backpacks of assorted sizes and shapes to claim your place under the sun—literally! The benches and seats on the deck are already taken, but you can claim your tiny share of real estate on the floor of the deck.

Once you've colonized your corner with your belongings, prepare for the sunrise on the Irrawaddy—a truly magical experience. For a moment, there is awed silence as the eastern sky starts blushing. Soon, almost every passenger on board is treading on your toes and tripping over your backpack to get a vantage view of the fishing boats against the rising sun.

The undulating surface of the river is slowly turning into a million shards of silver; yonder, fishing boats are silhouetted against the glowing fireball; the moment is almost magical. But then, the boat pitches and sways dangerously, threatening to capsize. If it does, you would be the first one off the deck. The awed silence of a moment ago is rent by shrieks and screams, and orders barked through the public address (PA) system by the captain urging you to get back to your seats. In the melee, the glorious sunrise goes unwatched, unappreciated and unphotographed.

As the sun travels up the sky and the boat moves at a slow but steady clip, you notice an unusual phenomenon on the foredeck. Two young lads are seated clutching the bow, and dipping two poles into the water, drawing them out and examining them, wiping the mud off, and again plunging them into the water. Initially it looks like they are amusing themselves. No, they have been employed by the ferry company to gauge the level of water in the river. Irrawaddy's sandbanks are legendary and so are the boats stuck in them. True to Asian jugaad, the captains have devised an ingenious system to take care of such eventualities. Why bother with sophisticated instruments for cattle ferries like this? Local boys are hired to sit on the foredeck with their graduated sticks that measure the depth of water as the boat sails along. It merely takes a shout from them for the captain to steer his vessel clear of the sandbank and scramble to safer waters.

The journey takes all of twelve languorous hours during which you loosen up completely. The only thing that is tightly wound up is your bladder, swelling to capacity and threatening to burst. The two toilets on the deck can put skunks to shame; they dare you to approach them, and naturally, you dare not.

The boat reaches Bagan at the twilight hour. The region's fabled *paya*s (Burmese for 'stupa' or 'pagoda') line up in a parade of ceremonial welcome. I have no prior hotel bookings nor any fixed itinerary in Bagan, and this is February, peak tourist season. But fear not, trust your trishaw driver to take you to a hotel to suit your budget.

In fact, no trip to Myanmar will be complete without a ride on that unique Burmese contraption called the trishaw. It is a bicycle with a sidecar attached and is designed for maximum discomfort, as much to the driver as to the passenger. But it comes in cheerful colours and with delightfully loquacious drivers who can regale you with local lore. The only catch is, your face is too close to the nether regions of the driver. With Burmese roads being what they are, frequent collisions of the risqué variety make the trishaw ride a tad spicy or dicey—depending on your preferences.

Myanmar might put Paris to shame when it comes to al fresco dining. Street cafes are popular with the locals who seem to have mastered the art of balancing their butts on those tiny plastic stools in bright colours. In the evenings, the street stalls and food carts do brisk business. If you stroll along the by-lanes after sunset, your olfactory senses will be assailed by the aroma of roasted sparrows, fried insects and other unfamiliar fare that might have been swimming, crawling, creeping only minutes ago. The Burmese slurp with relish these lip-smacking delicacies piled on heaps of steaming noodles, all under the glare of lights from colourful paper lanterns slung from tree branches. If you're brave enough to balance yourself on those stools, you might even relish the authentic Burmese fare provided you have not visited the local market. I had taken a stroll through the bazaar the previous evening and was struck by the live specimens of fish, fowl and all kinds of creepy-crawlies eyeing me warily from their glass cases; these seem tame in comparison with the glazed stare of disembowelled snakes with blood congealed on them, invitingly arranged in handwoven baskets.

From May Kah Lar Guest House, you have a vantage view of life as it unfolds in Bagan. If you think you're in some remote hinterland, think again. The streets are chaotic. Ancient buses straight out of the British Raj come bearing down on you, their horns blaring, their tyres pulling in opposite directions like a pair of feuding bullocks pulling a cart. If you manage to jump out of the way, you will find yourself in the arms of pink-clad women, a whole gang of them; actually, they are nuns going about collecting alms for the day. They cluck and fuss over your bruised skin and go their way.

If you go looking for a Band-Aid, make sure you ask any shop, even those slung about with pots and pans. Myanmarese mom and pop stores must have been the forerunners of today's departmental stores and supermarkets rolled into one. The merchandise hawked can range from children's tricycles to medicines, groceries to utensils and everything in between.

In Bagan, the distinction between businesses and homes seems to blur as shops double as lounges for whole families to spend time together: women cleaning rice or sewing, children doing homework by Petromax lamps, menfolk in sarongs smoking *beedi*s. It is truly like stepping into a living, pulsating, yet sepia portrait.

2013

Thieves at the Equator

'You have been selected!' gushes the breathless airline attendant in her charming Spanish-accented English as I approach the boarding gate. Her English vocabulary exhausted, she then lapses into Spanish. I am mystified but also flattered about having been chosen for whatever it is. Visions of a free across-the-world trip for two as a gift from the airline race through my fevered mind. Meanwhile, she brings a colleague to enlighten me. He explains in unmistakable English that out of the 300-odd passengers bound from Quito to Miami on that flight, I have been singled out for reopening of my X-rayed and checked-in baggage, which had already entered the entrails of the aircraft. I am marched a mile to the aircraft by a uniformed attendant who even holds an umbrella to shield me from the drizzle. The suitcase is disgorged from the stationary plane's belly and laid out on a bench under its wings. A menacing sniffer dog is curled up under the bench, and two beefy security men signal me to open the locks.

I fumble for my keys in my cavernous handbag and manage to open my oversized suitcase overflowing with unwashed linen and the detritus of a three-week journey through the Galápagos Islands and the Amazon jungle. With gloved hands they patiently pull out each item of clothing, and all other debris squeezed into every inch of available space. Naturally, nothing suspicious is found— even the seashells I had smuggled out of Galápagos are ignored. Pushing toothpaste back into its tube is easier than putting all the stuff back into a suitcase. Eventually, we manage to close the yawning suitcase and lock it. I look up smugly at one of the security men and say, 'You didn't look into the false compartment at the bottom—I had hidden the cocaine packet there.' My friend who had accompanied me for the inspection pipes up and says tongue-in-cheek, 'They didn't even locate the two live iguanas we had smuggled in from Galápagos.' The security men blush and avert their eyes, and we get further emboldened. I pull out my camera and am about to shoot the whole scene. The security shoo us off back to the boarding gate.

It must have been a routine check targeted at anyone with an unfamiliar name. The sight of the calm sniffer dog dozing off under the bench must have already convinced them that there was no contraband in the suitcase, but nevertheless they had to go through the motions.

Quito's Mariscal Sucre International Airport has other surprises too. On another occasion, while we were waiting to board a flight to Guayaquil (pronounced 'oyyakil') there is some commotion as a few men in apple-green uniforms enter the boarding area. Everyone clambers to get a better view and cameras are out, flashes pop. At first we think these must be footballers; only they attract such adulation in Latin America. My journalist friend goes to investigate and finds it is Rafael Correa, the Ecuadorian President, no less. She sidles up to him, takes a selfie with him and tells him she had written about his policies in her newspaper. He is surprised but moves on after exchanging pleasantries. We found out that he was flying in his own presidential aircraft. After about ten minutes, a plainclothesman, obviously an intelligence official, approaches us and shepherds us to an anteroom where begins a long inquisition to find out exactly what we were doing in that country and even what we had written about his president. It was by no means a friendly inquisition. We emerge from this ordeal somewhat shaken.

Quito never ceases to surprise you. In the historic old town, the moment you point your camera to shoot the city square or its gorgeous basilicas and churches, a cop in uniform materializes, asking you to put your camera back into your bag. No, he has no objection to photography, but he is worried that your camera will be snatched! Our hotel manager had warned us against carrying our passports or too much cash as we went sightseeing. Apparently, passport snatching is quite common, and photographs are morphed and the passports reused! Only in Quito can you witness the comic sight of foreign visitors hanging their backpacks on their front for fear of it being knifed if hung on the back. Quito's streets are awash with cops; in fact, there are more cops than tourists in the old town.

But we manage. In fact, more than manage. We take a public bus to the Equator Monument about an hour's ride away. It is more crowded than a DTC bus at peak hour and we clutch our bags as if our lives depend on it. At Mitad del Mundo, we stand triumphantly with one foot on either side of the metallic line which is actually a good 400 metres off the equator if you believe your GPS.

Quito is a quintessential Andean city, perched at a height of more than 9300 feet with a spectacular range running along its spine. It shares the distinction of being the highest capital in the world alongside Bolivia's La Paz. Quito's winding and sloping streets remind me of old town Leh. During different periods of history, Quito has been ruled by Colombians, Peruvians and others, but no one vandalized the local Quechua culture as much as the Spanish who colonized this part of the world in the sixteenth century. The imperialists went about systematically decimating and obliterating everything Ecuadorian. What remains today is only gilded Spanish churches plated with Inca gold and a hotchpotch culture of the Mestizos in the highlands. Not a single Inca structure remains. No wonder neighbouring Peru managed to tout Machu Picchu as one of the wonders of the world while all Ecuador can do is cling to its natural wonders—the Amazon jungle and the Galápagos Islands.

Even if the Spanish had not destroyed Incan vestiges, the many volcanoes that overlook Quito might have. On a clear day, one can see the towering Cotopaxi, the world's tallest live volcano, in its powdery snow crown. For some centuries it has remained dormant, but how long it will remain benign is a matter of speculation. Pichincha, the other volcano to which you can ride a téléphérique, erupted as late as August 2006. There are a few other minor fiery deities that had erupted sometime or the other in the past, some still smoking. In fact, the pan-American highway that leads south from Quito all the way to Patagonia is referred to as the Avenue of Volcanoes. Yet, Quiteños carry on stoically.

2005

Roman Holiday

Rome is charmingly chaotic, if you know what I mean. The other European cities are orderly, disciplined, peaceful and predictably dull, but Rome, delightfully, is none of these. It is almost like home turf for us Indians. The traffic is unruly and wilful, the pedestrians nonchalant, tourists weave in and out of all those crumbling ruins taking photos as traffic snarls and honks. Rome's familiarity has a way of making you unwind so completely that you lose all self-control.

And wisdom too, as I discover to my chagrin when I impulsively extend my stay in Rome on one of my official trips. It is only when I go looking for rooms to stay that I realize what I have gotten into, in the midst of summer holiday season in a city invaded by every teenager from across the Atlantic, the city ringing out with nasal Yankee accents, escalator handles and park benches stuck with chewed gum in psychedelic hues.

Someone tells me there's a counter in Roma Termini which books rooms for tourists. I head to the station with my suitcase only to find a sea of youthful humanity with the same purpose and intention. I join the serpentine queue in front of the counter and wait my turn.

Almost when it is my turn at the counter, it is snapped shut. 'Scusa' says a hand-scrawled placard, announcing that no more beds are available that night. The queue collapses into a heap on the floor of the station in a tangle of limbs and backpacks. I have no option but to follow suit. I shove my suitcase into the locker in the station and come back to join the sprawl on the platform. After a few hours, I even manage to doze off.

Around midnight, I am rudely woken by a few limbs tripping over me. There is a mad rush for the station gates as the limbs and backpacks reassemble and head out in haste. Roma Termini closes at midnight and everyone is shooed out. I too stumble my way out of the station and am promptly mobbed by waiting touts with offers of beds for the night. The rate starts at €120 for a night—depends on your level of desperation. The teenagers are ignored—they are never going to pay that much. In fact, they flop outside the station wherever they can find a spot. The touts then focus on the few people who are potential paying prey, including middle-aged me!

I pick one of them who seems less threatening and we haggle quite a bit—these touts are multilingual—and finally settle on €60 for a bed for whatever is left of that night. He first collects his cash, then marches me outside the station and we hop into his tiny car parked somewhere in the dark recesses outside. Off we go driving around the darkened alleys and lanes of Rome on a hot July night.

After about fifteen minutes of peregrinations through the streets frequented by dozens of drunks and streetwalkers in stilettos and net stockings, we reach an imposing gate. Alessandro, the tout, jumps out of the car, fishes out an impressive key bunch from his pocket and unlocks the gate, the first in a series that we would have to unlock and lock, like in the Arab tales of *A Thousand and One Nights*. After the second one, I feel I have already crossed the point of no return. With rising apprehension, which I hope is not evident in my tone, I ask, 'How much farther?' but Alessandro waves me off. Eventually, we reach the outhouse of a formidable mansion where the last door is unlocked. By now, my heart is pounding so fast I can hardly see where we are going.

We enter through the kitchen. A woman is cleaning the floor at this late hour. There are three shut doors, presumably leading to three bedrooms. There is a 4-foot sofa in the kitchen which Alessandro gestures me to occupy. Sixty euro for this? My anxiety has morphed into anger. I try to argue with him, but he shushes me and points up. There, in the half loft that covers the kitchen, two bodies are sprawled, mild snores emanating from one of them.

I resign myself to spending the night on the couch, my head and feet sticking out uncomfortably. Alessandro's wife, a Polish woman as I would find out later, tells me I must be up at six since it would be breakfast time for the lodgers. It is already past one in the night!

Early in the morning, I am rudely shaken awake by the mistress of this mansion, the same cleaning woman of the previous night. She directs me to one of the bedrooms through a tall door that is now open. My eyes pop out as I spy at least a dozen people sleeping in bunks and beds crammed into the space. She gestures, signalling I should lie on a bed just vacated by one of the lodgers, still warm and crumpled. I refuse and march back to the kitchen where my 4-foot sofa is now occupied by a couple of lodgers awaiting breakfast.

Alessandro's house has three bedrooms, of which two are crammed with bunks and beds. I count eleven beds in one bedroom; there must have been a similar number in the other, not counting the two in the kitchen loft. The middle room is occupied by Alessandro and his family comprising wife and three kids. Every inch of space in the house seems to have been used to accommodate hapless stranded souls like me. This is very lucrative business for Alessandro and his wife.

I pick up my bag and leave, looking for some Italian coffee to clear my clouded and confounded brain. The day is spent at the Sistine Chapel, braving the crowds and clicks, but a welcome relief from the trauma of the previous night. Michelangelo has worked his magic on the ceiling of the chapel, transporting you into another era where angels and saints flew through the skies in clusters. Images of teeming humanity portrayed in its naked weaknesses and indestructible strengths and God with His ability to transform everything and accomplish anything come alive from its walls and ceiling to haunt you for weeks. It is truly a feast of frescoes—throbbing, alive, forceful, vital and exuding inexhaustible energy.

Michelangelo's *The Creation of Adam* has endured in the imagination of generations of art lovers and critics—the most photographed, the most easily recognized of the Sistine Chapel frescoes. The sense of life flowing from a bearded God's fingers into humanity through Adam is a stunning depiction of Creation, of elevating man from a supine, listless creature into one electrified by vitality, energy and immense power. The physical perfection of both God—with his muscles thrusting under his robes, his intent gaze and his flowing beard—and Adam—a picture of innocence, untainted by sin as yet—are so evocative. The outstretched fingers barely touch; one can almost see the spark that ignites mankind; the moment is suspended in eternity and conveys the effect of dynamic, palpable tension.

Later that evening, I decide to go to Pompeii hoping to find rooms in Naples, which surely must be much less crowded. There are far more glamorous places in Italy—Venice, Pisa or Florence—for the young horde to descend on. Pompeii would not be on their bucket list, I hope. I head back to the dreaded Roma Termini to board a train to Naples.

You've heard of intelligent machines, but have you encountered any? Well, you would, at Roma Termini. Every time you ask for a ticket to any destination on Trenitalia, the vending machine invariably displays the most expensive train and ticket options. For instance, when you query for a ticket from Rome to Florence, it would offer you a couchette on the long-distance Eurostar to Venice, although the journey time between Rome and Florence is just two hours! After you've coughed up the extortionate fare and picked up the ticket spat out by the machine, it will display all the other options, the cheapest being just a quarter of the fare you just paid! My search for a ticket to Naples, also two hours away from Rome, throws up a couchette ticket on a long-distance train going south through Rome. It even includes a ferry ride to the Isle of Capri where I have no intention of going. I pay up, having woken up to the ways of intelligent ticketing machines only later.

I just about manage to lug myself through the vestibule and locate my fancy couchette and we're already chugging into Naples with its familiar and comforting architecture—multi-storied matchbox-like buildings with laundry fluttering in the balconies. If you still don't feel at home, step into the toilet at Naples station where you're guaranteed to.

The helpful rooms counter attendant at Naples station points me to an imposing and ornate rococo building just a few hundred metres across the station entrance. Awestruck, I query about the price. He shrugs his shoulders and says it should be okay. I am very impressed, even excited. I can go back home and boast how I stayed in the grand palace of the Medicis in Naples, never mind the Medicis never came this far and my history is half-baked. It is an ornate mansion with a flaring central staircase like in Bollywood movies of yore, curving balustrades and curling columns from which concrete cherubs hang precariously.

As I gingerly ascend the grand staircase and reach the top, I find there's hardly anything behind this grand facade—mostly demolished rooms, fallen beams and debris scattered everywhere. On the left wing, there seem to be some rooms intact, accessed through carved wooden doors at least 10 feet high. The doors are slightly ajar. I knock and enter. Lounging in reclining sofas, surrounded by frilly cushions, are an octogenarian couple, or so I believe, from their wizened visages.

Their room could be straight out of a period film: French windows, exquisite glass chandeliers, Victorian bric-a-brac, stained-glass bowls and vases, lace curtains, the works. Before I can ask them about renting a room in their mansion, the old man nods, springs out of his sofa like an agile teenager and briskly leads me down a long corridor strewn with more debris. At the other end, there is a biggish room, also embellished and ornate, with a four-poster bed in the centre. He then draws a twenty-five in the air. I ask, '25 euro?' He beams and nods. I look around for a bathroom—there is none to be found. I mime a shower and bathing and he leads me to another corner behind the staircase and throws open yet another pair of over-embellished doors that lead to an elaborate bath and WC.

If you think all this is a great bargain for €25, think again. There's constant banging and breaking, machine drills and construction noise to put up with. Besides, the couple speaks no English whatsoever. They were bound to be no help in navigating Naples. When I ask them about timings to visit the ruins of Pompeii, they stare in utter incomprehension. Perhaps they think I am haggling. She shakes her head vigorously in the negative. He, like all Italians, is expansively expressive. He lets loose a volley in Italian, shrugs his shoulders and gesticulates. Now my turn. I too nod, gesticulate violently, turn on my heels and go down the overwrought staircase in search of another hotel.

2016

Riding with the King

The knotted black bundle under our feet heaves rhythmically as the occupant seems resigned to its fate of being trapped in a bag. But then, every now and then, our vehicle hits a bump, causing the bag to jerk and twitch. We hold our breath, keep our feet safely up and away from the bundle and hope we do not get into any accident that would throw up consequences similar to those faced by Pi Patel in *Life of Pi*.

In fact, the consequences could be even worse in this case, considering we are travelling with a live, 11-foot-long king cobra, rudely interrupted in its quest for a mate. The bag in which it is coiled up is made of cotton cloth and nothing more. Its fangs can easily reach out to lacerate and inject its infamous venom into any limb that strays close enough. As if guessing my thoughts, our companion on this dangerous journey, Ram Prasad Rao, turns to me and says they do not stock antivenom serum for a king cobra bite. Very comforting indeed!

My friend V and I are accompanying Ram Prasad Rao and Ajay Giri, both researchers at the Agumbe Rainforest Research Station (ARRS), on a cobra rescue mission. The previous day, as we had landed at the ARRS, tucked away in a rainforest on the outskirts of a small village called Agumbe, in the Western Ghats, some 60 km from Udupi in Karnataka, we were told that there was little chance of spotting a king cobra in the wild; that king cobras were shy creatures who preferred to make themselves 'invisible' except when hungry or overcome by the urge to find a mate. Disappointed, we had shuffled through the research station where we were shown honeybees building hives and dracos climbing areca nut palms.

Even as we were wondering whether the visit was worth the effort of travelling more than a thousand kilometres, the ARRS got a rescue call. A live king cobra had been spotted entering a house in Kellur village, some 15 km from the research station. In fact, the village residents had seen two of the species in the adjacent fields, headbutting each other, a typical ritualistic combat between male cobras fighting for the right to mate. Mating season starts in earnest around end March, but fortunately for us, there are a few impatient males about even in February! We happily accompany Ajay and Ram Prasad Rao on their rescue mission. By the time we reach Kellur, it is dusk.

The entire village has turned up outside the house to watch the rescue.

There is an open well with no embankment where the cobra is hiding. If it slithered into the well, not only would it be very difficult to rescue it, but it might also render the well water unusable. As our rescue team arrives in Kellur, everyone is cautioned against going anywhere near the open well, which is difficult to spot in the dark. Ajay skirts the well with his hook, locates the reptile, expertly hooks it and drags it away from the well. All this happens in a split second even before we realize what is happening. Ajay has been working at the ARRS for the past six years and specializes in king cobras. He wears an infrared torch in a band around his head. Flashlights can confuse the reptile.

It takes Ajay quite a while to coax the reptile into a long cylindrical bag he has brought for the purpose. He lifts the snake with his hook and holds its rear end in his hands, trying to guide its face towards the opening of the bag. But the snake has other plans. It turns right back, forcing Ajay to drop it. King cobras have a long striking range. The snake turns away from the bag and goes looking for somewhere to hide. Its skin is a dull brown with bands. It is easily distracted by camera flashbulbs and torch beams. So we are told to switch off all lights.

Now it is pitch-dark save the infrared light on Ajay's forehead. There is an eerie silence and even Ajay moves stealthily so that he does not upset the reptile. Of course, snakes have no ears, they cannot hear, and this one, despite being in the prime of its life, seems to have weak eyesight too. Or, it is simply confused. Yet, there is not a trace of aggression in it. The ominous hood remains unopened, which is a good indication that the animal is not panicking—at least, not yet. But I am unable to resist the temptation to click. Naturally, my flashlight confuses and then provokes the snake into opening its hood in the classical cobra posture. This is a danger signal for Ajay. Now he has to be very careful. The king cobra is in an aggressive mood and might strike.

But not all king cobra bites are venomous, Ram Prasad Rao explains to me later. Fewer than 20 per cent of the bites carry venom. After all, it takes several weeks for the venom glands to secrete the venom and the king cobra would not want to waste it unless it feels absolutely threatened. Cobras seem to have a mechanism by which they can withhold venom even as they bite. No wonder then that despite the density of their population in the Western Ghats, king cobra bites are rare.

But all this knowledge is little comfort when you are confronted by an agitated and aggressive king cobra dazzling you with its expanded hood. Ajay keeps his cool. Eventually, the cobra backs down and slithers into the waiting bag. As soon as its tail disappears into the cavernous bag, Ajay pulls the string to close its mouth. Then he and Ram Prasad Rao use a stick to gently guide the snake into the interior portion of the bag. With the stick in place to keep the cobra from springing back, Ajay flattens the top half of the bag, knots it tight leaving little room for manoeuvre. Then they hoist the knot with the stick and gingerly carry the bag and deposit it in a corner of the yard. The relieved villagers crowd around Ajay, the hero of the moment.

We then go looking for the rival male reptile, but it is nowhere to be seen. The female, over whom the two fought, must be hiding in an abandoned termite mound, we are told. The female is usually smaller than the male and does not risk her life when titans clash over the right to mate with her. Males are attracted by the pheromones the female secretes during the mating season.

On the way back in the car, with the magnificent serpent curled up under our feet, Ajay tells us about his many encounters with king cobras. Our rescue mission ends with the release of the king cobra into the wilderness. Ajay locates an uninhabited wood, carries the bagged snake and releases the knot. At first, the reptile is confused but soon slithers out and makes for the bush. In a jiffy it is on the fence, its gleaming body glinting in the flash of phone cameras. It raises its head and watches for a while before disappearing into the darkness.

Mekong Diary

'Why Mekong?' asks S when I tell her of my plan to sail up the river. 'Why not?' I ask. 'Isn't it the spine of Asia? Hurtling down from the highlands of Tibet, the river courses through five countries before it reaches the South China Sea, some 4350 km away. Turbulent and untamed, this river has never been dammed, at least not yet. On its banks are some gorgeous towns: imperial Luang Prabang, stunning Angkor Wat, very French Vientiane and scores of smaller towns, all vibrant and sizzling with humanity. Besides, a sail up the Mekong throws up vignettes of life like no other.'

The filibuster is enough to rattle the resolute and the robust—what to speak of S, already seduced and ready to capitulate? From now on, it becomes easier. We both team up and use similar tactics to wear down two more friends:

R and RB. Now we are a nice foursome, important for the economics of a trip like this.

So, on a bright day, the four of us land in Ho Chi Minh City, the springboard for our ten-day adventure. Apart from obtaining visas for Vietnam, Cambodia and Laos, I had done little else by way of preparation for the trip, but did not let the other three get wind of it. I had been assured by a friend who used to work in Vietnam that it would be possible for us to hire a boat up the river, from a place called Chau Doc. I believed him.

We spend a couple of days in delightful HMC. If you think traffic in India is chaotic, go to Ho Chi Minh City to disabuse yourself. Scooterists weave in and out of traffic with unrivalled abandon even as dangling electric wires add a touch of danger and drama reminding me of our very own Ballimaran in Delhi. Vendor women with baskets of merchandise yoked from shoulder poles cross nonchalantly, not even glancing at the traffic lights that blink in utter confusion. We dodge traffic to visit the war museum, a sobering experience.

On day three, we go in search of a taxi, which would take us to Chau Doc some five hours away. After much haggling, we squeeze ourselves and our bags into a rickety jalopy sans air conditioning in this steamy weather. After a few minutes on the road, we suspect the vehicle doesn't have a clutch or gear either. We drive on, through dirt tracks, gullies, crowded villages and on to cattle ferries. We cross the Mekong five times—all on boats—before we are deposited in Chau Doc, in a heap of dislocated limbs and luggage.

You may struggle to locate Chau Doc on the map, but that doesn't deter the town from living it up. It is so lively you might believe you're in Piccadilly Circus or Montmartre. The wharf hums with dinghies and skiffs and boats of all sizes and denominations. Its streets festooned with colourful buntings, string lights, balloons and illuminated stars, Chau Doc seems all set for Christmas. Scooter-borne Santa Clauses wave cheerily, pedestrians jaywalk merrily, street food aromas mingle with the stench of sewers to tickle your olfactory nerves, young couples stroll hand in hand, licking ice cream from the same cone. Slung across the quay is an incongruity—an illuminated hammer and sickle, the symbol of Vietnam's ruling Communist party.

The riverbank is packed with locals: picnicking families, exercise freaks, walkers, cyclists and vendors hawking everything from boiled clams to balloons. We go find a hotel, dump our bags and head to the ferry terminal to book our tickets only to find that all ferries are fully booked by the ubiquitous European tourists. For the next two days, not a skiff is available; this is holiday season, we are told.

The other three plan a mutiny against me, but antagonizing me at this stage will have consequences. At least they think so, since they believe I have already made bookings in other Mekong towns. So they shut up and follow me, sulking away. We amble through the streets of

Chau Doc, stroll through its Corniche, watch fisherman fix nets, visit the numerous wats and offer incense, praying for an early ferry out of this town. We spend our days mostly on the riverbank, impressed by the extraordinary vibrancy of Asia which best manifests itself in a riverside town like this. RB samples every living, breathing insect and reptile on offer, the other three of us being vegetarians.

The interminable wait for a boat exposes my incompetence and cracks open fault lines in our friendship. Nothing tests friendship like being thrown together on a long trip. Much as I tried to explain to them how you don't need bookings in these remote riverside towns—in any case, that's what the guidebooks had told me—I knew I had lost their trust irredeemably.

Finally, our wish is granted on the third day when a compact boat becomes available. One condition though. The main cabin is occupied by sixty octogenarian French tourists, and all that we can occupy is the narrow stern where a few plastic chairs have been placed. The area is open to the elements. By now, we were so desperate we would have been happy to cling to the railing of the boat if need be. Soon we set sail, the foghorn blaring to clear the traffic.

I spy a little ladder leading up to the roof of the boat. Quietly I haul myself up, spread my shawl and surround myself with water and some snacks brought from Saravana Bhavan in Delhi. What bliss! My demure friends suffer the stuffy stern, too coy to see themselves clambering up.

Family outings on the Mekong, a cluttered waterway

The fog clears soon and Mekong reveals itself in all its glory. It is a congested waterway and the banks are alive with activity. In a while, it becomes very hot and humid, but I decide this rooftop perch is better than the stench in the stern, what with so many incontinent geriatric stomachs battling unfamiliar fare.

And from now on, we are treated to Asian riverine life at its rawest. Little boats sell everything from pots and pans, flowers, veggies, fruits and baskets of fowl and fish. There is a skiff rowed by two young boys, laden with snakes, many dangling on the side and some writhing on the floor of the boat. Apparently a delicacy in these parts.

The banks are a voyeur's delight. Old men in sarongs lounge outside floating homes, smoking cigarettes or playing mah-jong. Mothers bathe their infants on the ledges of their wattle homes while other women are bathing themselves, doing their laundry or washing kitchen utensils. There are boat-repair shops and cycle-repair shops, all perched precariously on wattle and bamboo platforms jutting into the river. There are even small factories with smoke curling out of the chimneys, and a few schools; we spy herdsmen herding their flocks of ducks and geese on the river; families travelling to their destinations on their own little canoes; fishermen hunched over their catch. In fact, fishing nets are a ubiquitous sight throughout the stretch; the hauls could range from sardines to eels and coils of river snakes. The river is said to be replete with otters and dolphins, but we do not see any. Every now and then, settlements fade away and wavy rice paddies take over.

After about eight hours of sailing, we reach Kaam Samnor, the immigration point for entry into Cambodia. It is a ramble of thatched shacks on an island. A few customs officials lounge under the shade of a tree. Empty beer cans and bottles litter the ground. All the romance of clearing immigration on the river evaporates as we sweat it out in the sultry sheds. It takes three hours for the officials to rouse themselves from their post-lunch stupor and attend to us. Finally, the sun is about to set when our passports are stamped and we are off.

Dusk invests Phnom Penh with an ethereal beauty; its banks sculpted with scenes from the famous Manthan— devas churning the ocean with Vasuki, the serpent—are silhouetted beautifully. Glittering wats line up on the banks as if in ceremonial welcome. The French tour group is finally rousing itself from its somnolence to get a glimpse of the magical moment as we dock in the Cambodian capital. We eye the French tourists wistfully. A gleaming Volvo bus is waiting for them at the jetty and they will soon be whisked straight away to Siem Reap, while we have to lug our bags and go looking for a hotel for the night. Ignoring the reproachful glower of my friends, I pull out a map and walk purposefully into the hotel opposite, a run-down seedy lifeless pad, and book two rooms for the night. And then I begin making inquiries about how to reach Siem Reap where the magnificent Angkor Wat is located.

Devas churning the Mekong with Vasuki offer a ceremonial welcome to visitors coming in to Phnom Penh by the river

I would love to sail up to Siem Reap. It would be a fitting tribute to an ancient civilization that built this stunningly aesthetic architectural marvel, the world's largest temple complex, primarily because of its ability to harness the waters of the Mekong. However, we discover that the river is no longer navigable from this point on and that we must take a bus to Angkor Wat.

The Angkor complex, situated on a 200-square-km area on the floodplains of the Tonlé Sap lake at the foot of the Kulen mountains, was the seat of a very advanced civilization presided over by the Khmer Empire between the ninth and fifteenth centuries. Dedicated to the Hindu god Vishnu, this temple complex is the largest among all places of worship founded anywhere in the world. Angkor was also the centre of the largest pre-industrial urban sprawl known to man. Contrary to popular perception, Angkor Wat is not a single monument, but one—perhaps the grandest—of the many temple complexes that dot the large area. The Angkor monuments dazzle us with their perfection and symmetry, harmony and symbolism and, above all, their scale and size.

Who could have dreamt up such an ambitious monument and how did they manage to build it in a pre-industrial age? Why should a temple dedicated to Hindu gods be built in Cambodia, where Hinduism subsists only in stone today, and not on the Indian subcontinent, where it was born?

Piecing together information culled from various sources, historians found an answer to the second question.

Kambujadesa—mangled into 'Cambodia' by European colonizers who found it a tongue-twister—was established by a valiant Hindu king who had his origins in India. The earliest mention of this theory is found in Chinese records, which refer to Kambujadesa as Funan, an Indianized settlement in South East Asia. Chinese accounts have been corroborated by Sanskrit versions, which state that a king, possibly from the Chola dynasty, married a Naga princess who ruled over Tonlé Sap and settled down in today's Cambodia to found a kingdom in the early centuries of the Christian era.

According to researchers, the Khmer Empire flourished because of its ability to alter the course of the Siem Reap River and harness its waters, but fell eventually because nature triumphed over man's ingenuity and reclaimed control. This precipitated the decline of the Khmer Empire, which was no longer immune to floods and drought, the blight of its neighbouring kingdoms in Asia.

After three days in Siem Reap admiring the ruins of Angkor Wat, we go back to the river to find a ferry to take us to Laos, only to discover that upstream, the river is full of cascades and is dangerous. My secret is already out and the other three prevail over me, marching me to the airport to try for a ticket to Vientiane or Luang Prabang, both in Laos. Luckily, tickets are available and we hop on to the tiny aircraft headed to Luang Prabang, a town like no other.

Lying at the confluence of two mighty rivers—the Mekong and the Nam Khan—Luang Prabang, the former imperial capital of Laos, belies the notion that the East and West can never meet. It is a felicitous blend of two very different cultures, the French and the Buddhist, and is perfectly at ease with this hybrid identity. Luang Prabang's high street is lined with trendy street cafes in the best tradition of their Parisian counterparts. Yet, the street is also home to splendid Buddhist wats and monasteries with gilded pagodas and glittering Buddha statues. The delicious aroma of freshly baked baguettes and croissants and the strong smell of dark-roasted coffee mingle with the heady fragrance of jasmine and parijaat garlands waiting to adorn the deities in the numerous temples that dot this town.

We spend a few days in this languorous land of the lotus-eaters, where everyone smiles beatifically. Orange-robed monks come by at dawn to collect their alms from devotees who line the street with offerings. We too join the lot, with rice cakes bought from street vendors. This daily ritual is so solemn and somehow defines Luang Prabang more than the wats and palaces. Yet, later in the day, you spot the same monks whizzing through the streets on their bikes, talking on their cell phones. This is Luang Prabang for you, perfectly at ease with its Janus face.

2006

'What in Heaven's Name Brought You to Casablanca?'

Our trip to Morocco was an afterthought, an impulsive, unscientific decision based purely on cartography. Just because the map revealed Morocco to be just a ferry ride away from the Andalusian coast where we were attending a conference, my friend R and I decided to extend our trip to this glamorous North African destination. Beyond obtaining a visa for Morocco before leaving Delhi, we had done little research, leaving everything else to the trusty old *Lonely Planet* guide—in this case, a dusty and literally old copy I had fished out from the dark recesses of my shelf.

Our peregrinations through Andalusia over, we end up in Algeciras on the Mediterranean coast of Spain, dump our bags in the locker at the ferry terminal and board a cattle ferry that would take us across the Straits of Gibraltar to Tangiers in Morocco. En route, it calls at Gibraltar, that glitzy and glamorous British outpost better known for being the location where the James Bond opus, *The Living Daylights*, was shot. Not having a British visa, we have to be content with gaping at the Rock from the decks of our Comarit ferry.

All five hours I stand on the deck, craning my neck for the first sight of the African coastline. When we pull into the Tangiers terminal, it is crowded enough to give us a hint of what lies ahead. But we are oblivious, in our hubris of heading to Africa, even if it is only Berber, not African Africa. When we reach the railway station, it seems like a mini Kumbh Mela. There is a sea of backpacking humanity sprawled all over the place, even on the floor, blocking access to the ticket counter. *Lonely Planet* had assured us that there were trains from Tangiers to magical Marrakech, romantic Casablanca and exotic Fes. I traipse over stretched limbs and strewn luggage to access the ticket counter at the far end. The only tickets available are two seats in an overnight train to Fes. I have to make a split-second decision whether to take it or go looking for lodgings in Tangiers.

And having made it, I have all night to rue my decision. Our ladies' cabin has four berths and eight veiled women crammed inside beside fifty-odd pieces of luggage in all denominations and shapes. I nod off fitfully on the hijab-covered shoulder of my neighbour. Every time the train jerks me awake, I glimpse a hennaed hand or bejewelled ankle poking through the hijab. The train deposits us at Fes station in the morning; we're all bleary-eyed and dazed.

At the station, we are mobbed by touts, all of whom converge on us wanting to escort us to the fanciest *riad* (traditional houses) in town. But we are armed. We wave the copy of *Lonely Planet* on their faces and lo and behold, they vanish like vampires shown garlic. Don't they know the types who would haggle over every dirham, armed with a dog-eared copy of yesteryears' guide? We hail a cab and head to the Medina to look for a hotel. Didn't *Lonely Planet* advise us to stay in the labyrinth for a better appreciation of Fes?

The oldest of Morocco's imperial cities, Fes was where Morocco as a political entity was born more than 1200 years ago. Everyone goes to Fes to glimpse the real Morocco of narrow alleyways inaccessible to motorcars, and to photograph its sprawling tanneries that produce some of the finest leather in the world. Moors, Berbers, Jews, Turks and Christians mingle in its bazaars, trading in the finest goods of their time. The Medina of Fes is a confusing labyrinth of 8000 lanes and gullies that would confound even local residents. But we are undeterred, even though this was pre–Google Maps era. The cheapest pension recommended by our guide looks a bit seedy, so we decide to try the next one, which seems even seedier. The third one seems less so, but has no vacancies. As we tick off the list one by one, we find that each new hotel we check out turns out to be pokier and seedier than the earlier one. Worse, even these are fully booked. It is getting rather late—it is already quite dark—and we're deep into the maze of alleys. I am not sure we can find our way out of here even if we wanted to.

Therefore, we decide to take the next one, however dreadful it might be. Pension Tala is perched on a terrace and boasts terrace views—of other similar pensions no doubt! We poke our head into the cave-like, winding metallic stairwell and shout into the gloom inquiring if rooms are available. To our surprise and delight, a disembodied voice answers in the affirmative. We pick up our backpacks and go in search of the voice, feeling our way through the narrow winding staircase.

The reception is a hole in the wall on one side of the stairwell. But that's not the problem. To reach the reception, I have to plaster myself like a lizard on the wall and shinny up to the entrance. And having entered, I find that the roof is so low that I—all of 5'4"—have to kneel. There are three other backpackers already kneeling or squatting before the reception desk—which is a low stool on the floor! They look at me in dismay, wondering whether I am a threat to their claim to a room in this pigeonhole of a pension! But after two hours of loitering in the winding alleys of Fes, we're truly grateful for a bed even if it is in a windowless dungeon. After all, we came to this heritage town only for the authentic Fes experience!

Fes may be a magnet for the sanitized Western tourist who finds everything exotic, but only too familiar to the jaded Indian eye. Its labyrinthine lanes remind us of the streets of Agra or Mughalsarai, its numerous dye vats not unlike those in the back alleys of Chandni Chowk. We wander through the dark, dungeon-like alleys where the bluest of blue skies appear like narrow ribbons between buildings, chequered by dangling electric lines; we clench our noses to escape the fragrance of tanning leather, pick our way through dye vats that stain not only the fabled Moroccan leather but also the streets and walls of Fes, duck under clothes lines slung about with washed bed linen from the hundreds of pensions that dot the town, and dodge the ubiquitous donkey carts piled with merchandise or, sometimes, just rubbish. And yet, despite the familiarity or perhaps because of it, there is an irresistible charm to Fes. It transports you to a bygone era.

From Fes, we head to Casablanca, also by train. For those of us on the wrong side of fifty, the mention of Casablanca brings alive black-and-white images of that electrifying pair, Humphrey Bogart and Ingrid Bergman, exquisite in their 1940s outfits. But don't go to Casablanca with stars in your eyes and nostalgia tugging at your heart. Now it is a modern city that has little that is 'black-and-white'. There are colourful banners and posters advertising the latest designer ware or perfumes. A sprawling metropolis more European than Madrid or Naples, Casablanca seems to be going through an identity crisis. The picture-book emerald palm trees that lined the streets like soldiers in a parade are still there, but so are the art-deco buildings and designer-ware shops, the homes of the ultra-rich with their manicured lawns and sparkling swimming pools. Whoever would say Casablanca is in Africa? This seems more like Costa del Sol on the other side of the Mediterranean—in Spain, or the California coast.

Well that may be because I had preconceived notions of Africa—of ebony-skinned, curly-haired, statuesque men and women in chunky bone and horn jewellery and colourful bandanas, souks heaped high with spices, endless stretches of sand interspersed with lush jungles and untamed rivers and hordes of wildebeest seen only on National Geographic channels, etc. Banish the thought. Morocco is hybrid, neither African nor European, and yet entirely metropolitan. The Phoenicians, Romans, Arabs, Portuguese and finally the French, all of whom have ruled Morocco at some time in the past, have surely left behind their genetic and cultural legacy.

On to this delightful melange is grafted modern Islamic architecture in the form of various palaces and mosques built by their beloved monarch, Hassan II. Our train from Marrakech deposits us at Casa-Voyageurs station. The jade minaret of the Hassan II mosque—the mother of all Moroccan sights—looms over the Atlantic coast. We hire a taxi and head for the mosque. Our drive takes us along the beach, which, on this working day morning, is so crowded, despite the relentless African sun! And along the beach are endless swimming pools, all of them choc-a-bloc, presumably with tourists! Vendors are selling baskets heaped with what seems like peanuts. On closer inspection, I find they are boiled clams! Our driver wants to show us the sights of Casablanca, especially the rich people's villas and mansions. When we ask to be taken to Bogart's Rick's Café, he takes us to Rex Café and insists the film was shot there.

The Hassan II mosque, built at a cost of $800 million to commemorate the monarch's sixtieth birthday in 1993, is the third largest in the world, while its jade minaret, at 210 metres, is ostentation in marble and granite. In true Casablanca style, the minaret adds a touch of drama when at night it sprays laser beams in the direction of Mecca. There is a steep entry fee of 120 dirhams (Rs 600), but who will grudge it when it comes with an English-speaking guide? You're overawed by the decor and the staggering expanse of the mosque—its esplanades alone can accommodate 80,000 worshippers. Once you cross its high-tech steel-girder suspended gates operated electronically, another 20,000 can be seated inside. I shut my eyes and visualize the esplanade on Id—all those fez-covered heads bowing in unison.

This mosque, which looks more like an ornate mall, was designed by the French architect Michel Pinseau and looks suitably French on the outside. It's only when you step inside that you realize how typically Moroccan the construction is—cedar wood from Middle Atlas, marble from Agadir and granite from Tafraout adorn its floors, walls, arches, columns and ceilings. As many as 6000 skilled craftsmen worked for years to complete this mosque which is more a statement than a place of worship. Naturally, there are more tourists about than worshippers. The mosque itself stands on an erstwhile slum whose residents are reported to have been evacuated without any compensation.

After a day in Casablanca, we decide to head to Marrakech, the sexy metropolis that midwifed the birth of the mighty World Trade Organization. We ditch our copy of *Lonely Planet* to heed the advice of a tout who zeroed in on us at the railway station. We check into the ornate Riad Fantasia that looks every bit as promising as its name sounds. It has a fine courtyard with exquisite tiles, swaying palms and a lovely fountain in the middle. The rooms are arranged around the leafy courtyard.

But external appearances can be deceptive, as we would soon find out. When I try to open the door of the bathroom, it swings violently from a hinge on top and crushes my finger. Not only does this bathroom door hang from the top to be pushed aside like a curtain to enter or exit, the arrangement also leaves a generous 6-inch gap between the wall and the door, offering a voyeuristic glimpse of the goings-on inside, not to mention the potent olfactory assault.

Soon we are on our way to the souk, the soul of Marrakech. It is where life happens. There is a profusion of merchandise artistically stacked and crying out for your attention and your emaciated wallet. Ubiquitous is the footwear, colourful and embroidered. Then you have the tassels, painted Berber ceramics and charming bric-a-brac, mostly stuff without which you can live your life happily forever!

Mohammed, the self-proclaimed double of Dr Zhivago, has a million vials of cosmetics in his shop. He proudly waves his cell phone in our face—it has Aishwarya Rai for wallpaper. Neatly arranged colourful jars brim with potions promising everything from eternal youth and beauty to cures for earache and herbs for slimming. With great reluctance, we extricate ourselves from the souk and head for the hammam—the public bath that has been upgraded to a spa, solely to fleece unwary tourists! The attendant speaks flawless English and the rates are commensurate with her linguistic felicity! But we deserve a bit of pampering—after all that shoving and pushing in the souk and getting slammed by a bathroom door dangling from the roof.

In the evening, we make our way to Jemaa el-Fnaa, the most happening place in Marrakech. The exotic ambience of sizzling street food is embellished by the presence of a colourful cast of characters—raconteurs of enchanting tales, snake charmers, musicians, magicians, masseurs, dancers and drummers—all make your evening memorable. We sip sweet mint tea in one of the many stalls that dot the square.

We take the ferry back to the Spanish coast. When we go to retrieve our luggage from the locker in Algeciras port, it gobbles up several euro but refuses to yield our luggage.

We go in search of an attendant; the one we find speaks no English whatsoever. Wild gesticulations and a volley of abuses in Tamil persuade him to accompany us to the locker rooms where he opens our locker, but charges €20 and gives us a receipt in Spanish. I pull out a paper from my suitcase, write out an elaborate complaint and drop it in what I presume is the suggestion box. I am yet to hear from them.

2006

The Impossible Trail of Nikitin

The babushka grumpily serves a bowl of buckwheat porridge accompanied by a naked teabag. This has been our breakfast for the past ten days. We are in Kazan, the capital of Tatarstan in the Russian heartland. This is only the fifth stop on our six-week-long road trip through six countries. It could only get progressively worse as we proceed through the neglected wastelands of the Russian steppe farther south.

We were on a grandiloquently named road trip called the Nikitin Expedition—ostensibly retracing Afanasy Nikitin's footsteps. As to who was Nikitin and why we were retracing his footsteps, I will come in a moment. The trip was a bungle from the word go. First of all, we set out in the wrong season when Russia was already heavily quilted in metre-thick snow. It was not meant to be so. We were to leave in July and return to India by August, but what with six visas for fourteen persons to be wangled free of cost out of sceptical diplomats, it got pushed to mid-November. Undeterred, we set out, a motley group of Indian scholars fluent in Russian and Persian, a renowned photographer (who wisely turned back from Moscow itself), a doctor, an attractive Kathak dancer, three film crew, one of them a sprightly young woman, a woman journalist and I. That made for four women in a group of fourteen. Mahindra had agreed to provide its SUVs to test them on Russian terrain. There were two drivers under the watchful eye of SK, their man on the trip. And all of us were shepherded by a retired bureaucrat—a glad-eyed and 'redoubtable' team leader who'd organized the trip.

Little did we realize that the only decent meals we would get on this historic journey were the in-flight fare dished out by the Aeroflot flight from Delhi to Moscow. Occasionally, we could get our teeth on bread and salt, offered by our hosts in frontier towns as a mark of traditional welcome. For the rest, it was largely cabbage salad and vodka for the two vegetarians on the trip.

The flight was teeming with fellow Indians, the lot that sends remittances to keep our foreign reserves afloat. I asked the thirty-something next to me where he was going. He had no clue. He was from Dubai, like the rest of the 140 on board, and they were being taken to another oil installation somewhere. He pulled out his ticket to show me. From Moscow, he would have to fly another eight to nine hours and cross several time zones to reach Sakhalin where temperatures must be plumbing the Arctic depths. They had no idea where they were going or what to expect except that they had been assured higher wages by their contractor. Coming from Dubai, they did not even have woollens to deal with the Delhi winter, leave alone Siberia. What was I complaining about, starting our expedition in winter?

Just before leaving Delhi, I was curious to find out who Nikitin was. It turned out he was a small-time Russian trader from the boondocks who decided to seek his fortune farther south, gliding his way down the Volga, trudging across the deserts of Iran and sailing east down the Persian Gulf and the Arabian Sea to land somewhere near Mangalore. He took eighteen months to reach India, and along the way, he was robbed, roughed up and ridiculed. He lived three years in western India and left copious, unflattering notes about the country and its denizens. Yet, Bollywood found him so irresistible that it roped in Balraj Sahni and Nargis to do a biopic on him, called *Pardesi*. It was then that I realized that it helps to have a theme, even Nikitin, when you go about raising funds for a venture like this.

We cooled our heels in a seedy hotel in St Petersburg for five days until the cars shipped by Mahindra reached the Baltic shores.

Mahindra SUVs lined up outside the Winter Palace in St Petersburg, ready to launch forth on the Nikitin expedition

We set off in three Scorpios, strikingly emblazoned with dozens of sponsors' logos, to reach a nondescript town called Tver, between St Petersburg and Moscow. Afanasy Nikitin is Tver's sole claim to fame. Surprisingly, some 700 Indians came out to greet us in Tver, all of them students at the local medical college. A Malayali was running a canteen for them on campus.

Later, we encountered similar crowds of students in virtually every Russian town we passed through. Medical education in Russia is cheap and non-discriminating. Our compatriots in most of these towns seemed ill-equipped to deal with the extreme snow they had to brave to earn a doubtful degree recognized by neither Russia nor India.

Russians do not trust their own patients with these doctors and the Medical Council of India insists they prove their medical proficiency all over again if they want to practise in India.

Our expedition was flagged off by a senior Indian diplomat in a blinding blizzard in Tver town square even as some expedition members swept the snow off Nikitin's statue for the photo op. In the freezing weather, we shook almost as much as the banners that were being unfurled, and took regulation photos. We were grateful to get back into the vehicles with frosted windows and blowers on. The Scorpios were our comfort zone for the next six weeks, for reasons even other than the weather.

We were to drive along the Volga for most of the time, until we parted company with it after Volgograd. The Volga has been the nerve centre of the Russian heartland—virtually all important Russian towns are perched on its banks. The roads we were now driving through must have seen tsars and tsarinas riding their grand white steeds, to be replaced by Lenin and Stalin's soldiers, marching on to change the course of world history. Napoleon and Hitler found a formidable adversary in the Russian winter, marching their troops along the Volga to meet their most humiliating defeat on its banks. Yet, our intrepid SUVs took on the same roads without the slightest trepidation and successfully completed the trip without a single breakdown, truly a testament as much to modern technology as to the manufacturer's attention to perfection.

The Volga, the silent sentinel who watched over the making and unmaking of Russia, sparkled in her white blanket. Completely frozen, it was a white ribbon of meandering snow alongside the road, its banks lined with poplars and pines whose needles had turned to icicles. Every town in Russia has its own kremlin, even if a bit diminutive compared to Moscow's. Their fortresses and the steeples of the many churches beckoned from the banks like fairy-tale castles in faraway lands.

The drive would take us from Tver to Moscow, Nizhny Novgorod, Muslim Kazan, Samara, Saratov, Volgograd, Kalmykia (a Buddhist Republic within the Russian Federation), Kropotkin (home of the Cossacks), Astrakhan on the Caspian and Sochi on the Black Sea.

Along the route, the Soviet-era hotels in which we stayed got seedier by the day. Invariably, our rooms would be on the fourth or higher floors, with dysfunctional elevators. The only breakfast we would get was kasha and tea. Many days, our team leader insisted on driving through without stopping for lunch on the pretext we were already late. Probably he was trying to keep expenses in check, but I would give him the benefit of the doubt since we were also tardy. He balked at the suggestion that we should get snow tyres—we skidded several times on metre-deep snow. Eventually, we prevailed upon him to prise open his purse strings for snow tyres, leaving him sulking all the way.

Tyre swallowed tarmac as we rolled through town after town, day after day. It was a surprise to spot exquisitely decorated gingerbread-style churches in the midst of the expansive and isolated landscape. The drive offered 360-degree horizons lit up by brilliant sunsets, bulrushes resonating with birdsong in some stretches, dreary wastelands and quaint villages.

Days were getting shorter as we rolled through the desolate steppes, reaching our destination for the day well after sunset. Often, we would spy a lone vehicle and a handful of locals in traditional costumes waiting for us in the middle of the highway as we rolled in three to four hours after the scheduled time. We would be whisked off to hour-long speeches by local dignitaries followed by never-ending cultural programmes showcasing local talent. There were dances in exquisite ceremonial costumes, lilting ballads, skits and sporting events, exchange of gifts and sashes—all executed with fitting gravitas and organized exclusively for our benefit. We would have enjoyed and appreciated them better had we not been exhausted and famished. Past midnight, we would troop back to our rooms and swig vodka to lull ourselves to sleep.

Eventually, all of us four women gravitated to the vehicle driven by SK, leaving our expedition leader fuming. SK was a miracle man who could balance with elan a movie camera in his right hand which would also somehow manage to steer, while his left would make tea with water from a thermos to keep himself awake during these long and monotonous drives. For us women, the solace lay in bottles of vodka which we quaffed in copious quantities to silence our rumbling stomachs.

The trip was not devoid of distractions though. In Kazan, whose population is 60 per cent Muslim, local girls in Kanchipuram saris twirled and twisted to offer us their version of Kalakshetra against the stark backdrop of the Russian steppe; elsewhere, Russian and Ukrainian beauties in sheer nylon sequinned saris gyrated to Bollywood ditties. In Saratov, we feasted on a bountiful collection of Nicholas Roerich's priceless Himalayan peaks. In Ulyanov, we marvelled at Lenin's simple home and gaped at his sepia-tinted ancestors. In Volgograd, a prosperous industrial town of the Soviet era, the factories had fallen silent and the chimney stacks of steel mills no longer sent up plumes of curling smoke. We were told unemployment is rife in this once flourishing town of historic importance. In Kalmykia, one of the two Buddhist republics in the Russian Federation, we chatted in Hindi with monks trained in Dharamshala. In Kropotkin, we pounced on the feast laid out by the hospitable Cossacks who were seeing Indians for the first time in their town. In Sochi, we planted saplings for Indo-Russian friendship.

Hotel Primorskaya, our last Russian hotel overlooking the Black Sea, had miles and miles of corridors with frayed and smelly carpets, chipped enamel fittings in toilets and a decadently decorated conference hall. All of the above was no surprise, except, this hotel was full of Russian devotees of Ma Anandamayi, her smiling visage beaming at us from every pillar and wall. The gathering was entirely Russian, the crowd solemn and serious—an incongruous sight in a largely secular post-Soviet Russia.

The Russian leg over, we set sail down the Black Sea in MV Apollonia to Turkey. Over a bottle of evil-smelling absinthe, the sufficiently sloshed captain informed us his passengers on this route were mostly 'Natashas' seeking their fortune in markets farther south. We realized he was talking about attractive Russian girls headed to brothels in Turkey and elsewhere. From Trabzon in Turkey, we climbed up the Caucasus to Georgia and just zipped through Tbilisi without stopping, to waste two hours listening to Azeri poetry in the dead of night at the tomb of a Persian poet called Nizami Ganjavi, shivering in blinding snow somewhere in the wildernesses of the Caucasus just because R, the only Persian speaker in our group, was too polite to tell our hosts we were getting late. Georgia, the land of the golden fleece in the Bible, is a beautifully mountainous country with its own unique architectural style. Georgian wines have taken over shelves all over the supermarkets of the West, although we didn't get to taste any.

Nearly a month after we had set out from St Petersburg, we entered Iran through the border check post of Astara, after an excruciating wait of three hours. All of us women had to don a hijab, preferably a burqa, but we made do with scarves. Of course we looked nothing like the Iranian women advertising their style by the cut and size of their manteaus. We looked woebegone by the travails of the journey thus far, but our spirits were up. Iran is a treasure trove waiting to be discovered and we were raring to go.

It was already evening by the time we reached our guest house which looked more like a student hostel. The lobby had a huge portrait of Iranian politician and *marja* Ayatollah Khomeini under which we all plonked ourselves and opened our vodka bottles smuggled all the way from Russia. Two of our women team members smoked an entire packet of cigarettes until the smoke curled up and clouded Khomeini's portrait. Our pictures taken under his frowning visage, we now looked forward to a warm and rewarding drive through Iran's gorgeous towns—Tabriz, Tehran, Isfahan, Shiraz.

But our team leader had other plans. Frustrated by what he thought were the wilful and recalcitrant women he had mistakenly roped into this road trip, he decided to teach us a lesson. He called off—yes, called off—the expedition in the middle of the highway from Astara, citing financial difficulties. He and some of the men in the team, including the three drivers, would proceed to complete the trip in the three Scorpios, while we four women were left high and dry in the middle of the Iranian desert to fend for ourselves. As a concession, R, the Persian speaker, was let go, so that he could steer us home by whatever means of transport.

Little did our insensitive and callous team leader realize it would take more than that to faze the four of us.

We hired a taxi from Tehran and whizzed alongside the expedition cars all the way to Isfahan and Shiraz, visited all the interesting mosques and mausoleums, *maqbara*s and madrasas, and flew back to Delhi, nearly seven weeks after we had set out. It was a strange experience to spot the expedition vehicles wherever we went, and yet be disconnected in every sense.

The epilogue is not to be missed. Months afterwards, long after the cars shipped from Bander Abbas arrived in Mumbai, the team leader had the gall to invite us women to participate in the last Indian leg of the expedition along the Konkan coast just so that he could complete his film for his sponsors. All of us gleefully declined. And with that, hopefully restored the peace of the traumatized Afanasy Nikitin kept awake in his grave by our botched-up expedition.

2005

Travails of a Vegetarian Traveller

The Lazy Susan swings slowly towards me. Atop are two inviting plates—one heaped with chunks of plump, juicy, steamed lotus stem, and the other piled high with blanched pak choi. I get ready, armed with a pair of chopsticks poised for attack; never mind I have never used this contraption before. I plunge the sharp edge of my chopsticks into the latticework of the lotus stem and hoist the piece triumphantly to my mouth. Before I can go for a second helping, my neighbour has already flicked the rotating disc towards himself and away from me. But never mind, it will come back, I console myself.

We are about a dozen people of different nationalities seated in a fancy restaurant in Beijing around a huge circular table. I am the lone vegetarian in the group. My immediate neighbours are a Russian on the left and a Chinese on the right, both fellow delegates at a conference, like everyone else around the table. Carrying on a conversation through the interpreter seated at the far end, even as you wrestle with the plate of delicacies on a perpetually rotating Lazy Susan, is enough to ruin anyone's appetite. But there is worse to come. In the next round, a new dish of boiled peanuts, incidentally my favourite, is added to the existing vegetable dishes. Try picking up a peanut with chopsticks while making distracted conversation with your neighbour without the aid of the interpreter who is busy with other delegates. Finally, when I do manage to pick up a recalcitrant nut with a pair of pincers and raise it to my lips, it changes its mind and rolls on to my neighbour's lap.

Meanwhile, the elegant waitresses in traditional Chinese silk gowns have gotten busy, piling the table with a procession of dishes. First comes a dish of slimy squid, followed by an impressive lobster with fearsome claws, which my fellow diners go on to dismember delicately and with practised ease. They savour the succulent limbs with evident pleasure. Then comes a full fish, eyes and gills intact, quite artistically done, one must admit, although I feel it is mocking me. This is followed by a plateful of whole pink chicken, legs folded just so; then comes a whole duck looking decked up with all those salads stuck on its sides. Finally arrives a whole piglet straight from the spit, its cute pink snout sizzling away seductively. Trust the Chinese to show the diners what exactly they are being served! I am grateful snakes are not on the menu today.

My Chinese neighbour expertly plunges his chopsticks and delicately picks out some gooey squid and stuffs it into his mouth without spilling a drop. Then he uses the same chopsticks to pick up the pak choi and the lotus stem, one after the other. So do the others, all of whom seem to be enjoying their meal immensely, even as I sit holding my breath to escape the unfamiliar aroma wafting from the dishes. The tips of their chopsticks plunge alternately into the fish, meat and the vegetables with equal ease. This is interspersed with shouts of '*Ganbay!*' as the diners tip tiny glasses of rice wine to wash down the meal. No one even notices that I am the only one not eating. I had requested the organizers to inform the restaurant in advance about my dietary peculiarities. They have obviously forgotten, what with so many things on their plates—pun unintended.

I sit back and watch my colleagues with as much fascination as resignation while my stomach rumbles and protests. Finally, I pluck up the courage to summon a waitress and request her, through the interpreter, to bring me a bowl of rice. She gives me a disgusted look and, in a moment, slaps a very small bowl of boiled rice, each grain as big as peanuts and almost as brown. After darting a furtive look at my fellow diners, all of whom are busy enjoying themselves, I stuff the rice into my mouth and chase it down with rice wine.

Well, it took me a few trips to realize that in China buffet meals are virtually unknown and banquets are de rigueur on official visits. So, during my next visit to the country,

I decide to skip the banquet hosted by the organizers and instead go into the restaurant to order a la carte. But the menu is all in Chinese. The maître d' brings an English-speaking assistant to understand my requirements. He beams, nods and bends in salutation and disappears behind the bamboo screen. In a little while the waiter appears with a plate heaped with boiled baby cabbage. Except, there is nothing babyish about the cabbage; it is as huge as it is slimy and I am unable to slice it even with a fork. When I try stuffing one end into my mouth, the rest hangs out of my face, making me look like a clumsy plant holder hit by a tropical storm. To slowly swallow the vegetable bit by bit requires quite a bit of gustatory gymnastics. With my dignity in tatters and my stomach still rumbling with rage, I exit the restaurant.

The next day, the baby cabbage exited my system whole and intact!

1997

Stumped in Paradise

In October 2016, I get a cold call on my cell phone. The voice at the other end says, 'My name is C. I wonder if that rings a bell.' Of course it does. The timbre of the voice, tucked away in the recesses of my memory, is unmistakable. It has been nineteen years since I last heard it, but how can I forget it? 'Major C?' I query. 'Well, make it Brigadier C, if you please.' Of course, how foolish of me! The next day, we meet at an army mess for lunch and it is then that Brigadier C opens up and finally reveals the answer to my query that had boggled my mind for years. He has retired from service and is settled in Gurgaon. He just got my number from a mutual friend and decided to surprise me. Our acquaintance goes back to 1997 when providence threw the two of us together on a dangerous car journey through desolate mountain roads in Kashmir on a beautiful moonlit night.

I was returning from the holy caves of Amarnath that fateful evening in July 1997. Those were still early days of the Amarnath Yatra. The previous year, I had undertaken a thirty-two-day trek to Kailash Mansarovar. The scenery was stunning and the experience exhilarating, so much so that it had whetted my appetite for more. So I had decided to check out the Amarnath trail the following year. It was a much shorter trek, ranging from six to eight days for a return trip. Being in Kashmir, it held out promise of jaw-dropping scenery as well. And so much cheaper too, since it didn't entail a $500 visa fees to the Chinese, which all Kailash *yatris*, or travellers, had to shell out. The Amarnath caves are well inside Indian territory, although Pakistan would like it otherwise.

I take a flight to Srinagar and hire a taxi up to Pahalgam. It is only when you arrive in Chandanwari near Pahalgam to begin your trek that you realize what you have let yourself in for. The scene is worse than Delhi's Sarojini Nagar market on the weekend before Diwali. Crowds are milling about on the slopes, often causing traffic jams. Porters, pony-wallahs, pilgrims and peddlers of assorted religious memorabilia jostle for space on the narrow trail. Sadhus with matted hair and skimpy loincloths march briskly even as you shiver under three layers of woollens. Self-styled traffic wardens try in vain to put some discipline into the yatris who seem to occupy every inch of the slope.

Dozens of langars of every denomination have sprung up, their banners proudly announcing their religious affiliations. Everything from Gujarati thali to rajma-rice and idli-dosa is on offer, all for free. Yatris can have multi-cuisine meals several times a day if they so desire. Religious organizations of multiple denominations vie with each other to stuff your face in order to earn their *punya*. Try as you will, resisting these gustatory seductions, there is no escape. Every few yards, samosas and laddus will be thrust into your hands, along with Tetra Pak mango drinks. Quietly you drop these, unopened and untasted, into the Lidder River that accompanies the trail. Naturally, the river is submerged in a deluge of discarded food, TetraPaks and snack wrappers. There is so much filth that the Lidder can easily put the Cooum in Chennai or the Yamuna in Delhi to shame. A word of warning to female yatris—I wasn't warned, but like a Good Samaritan, I am warning others. Practise bladder control for weeks before you venture out on this yatra. There is no female toilet anywhere until you reach camp six hours away, and nary a bush or shrub for you to hide behind. Men being from Mars, the sacred Lidder silently suffers their incontinent bladders. Women yatris can pretend not to notice and plod on, ignoring the overwhelming stench.

The first night, I stay in Sheshnag, where the devout believe a five-headed mythical serpent would emerge out of the emerald waters of the lake, if you can brave subzero temperatures and watch out all night. I opt for sleep instead. On day three, I am at the cave around noon. I pass through the newly installed metal detectors at the entrance.

The place is swarming with security personnel. After much pushing and shoving, darshan is over in a few minutes. I am back in the bazaar wondering how I am going to brave the crowds and my recalcitrant bladder for three more days on the return trek.

But first things first: lunch in one of the langars. After much deliberation, I pick the Marathi one and gorge on *sabudana* vadas and *missal pav*. Sated, I wander through the stalls that hawk assorted religious memorabilia. In one of the stalls, I inquire about the availability of alternative trails to Srinagar. A helpful shopkeeper comes to my rescue. 'Take the Baltal route. It is only around 10 km. You should reach in two or three hours. Srinagar is just two hours from there. But there are no camps or langars en route,' he warns.

That seemed incredible. Why does the official trekking trail take us through a circuitous Pahalgam route lasting three or four days? Why don't the yatris come or go via Baltal then, I ask him. 'Madam, the yatris want to go through Sheshnag for the chance to glimpse the holy serpent. Besides, the Baltal route is rather steep and only the fittest will be able to take it.' He remembered something else and continued, 'Also, you may not get transport from Baltal to Srinagar. Better you call your hotel in Srinagar and ask them to send you a taxi to Baltal.' The Baltal route goes along the Indus River and offers equally spectacular views as the Pahalgam route.

Cell phones had made their appearance in India only a couple of years ago and only the rich and snazzy used them. For the rest, there were the ubiquitous STD booths. I call my hotel in Srinagar where I have a booking for my return stay three days hence. Yes, they have a room that night and will send a taxi which should reach Baltal by 3 p.m. The helpful hotel staff give me the number of the taxi and the name of the driver. All tied up, I am on my way down.

In 1997, the Baltal route did not seem popular at all. A few sadhus and pony-wallahs are the only ones headed that way. The path is so steep I struggle to keep pace with these veterans. Apart from the sound made by the hooves of horses, this route is silent. No shouts of *'Jai Bhole Nath!'* or *'Bum Bum Bole!'* that rend the air on the other trail. The river along the trail is criss-crossed by a few rickety bridges and interspersed with impressive waterfalls. Although I had been assured I could reach in a couple of hours, I seem to go on for ever. By the time I reach Baltal, it is already dusk.

Baltal has a sprawling army camp, but no hotels. I spy a lone white Ambassador car parked under a tree. Ashraf, the elderly driver, is frowning, intently watching those who come down the slope. I approach him and introduce myself. He doesn't seem too happy to see me. 'Madam, it is already getting late. It would be better if we stay in the camp here tonight and leave early in the morning.' But I am impatient to get to Srinagar so that I can use my open ticket (yes, you had them in those days) to see if I could get on a Delhi-bound flight the next day. I insist we leave right away, without waiting for dinner. Ashraf sulks, clucks his tongue, and is about to say something. But he changes his mind and gets into the driver's seat. I hop into the rear and we roll out of Baltal.

We have traversed just a short distance through the army camp when two uniformed soldiers come running from the opposite direction and block our path. Ashraf stops the car and rolls down the window. They ignore him and approach my window, which I roll down too. 'Madam, Major saab wants to have a word with you.' Major saab? Who? Why? I am a bit confused. But I tell Ashraf to wait, and am about to get out of the car. Meanwhile, a tall and handsome young officer in uniform, the Major saab, comes at a brisk stride towards me, bends down and greets me. 'Good evening, ma'am. Are you going to Srinagar?' I nod in the affirmative, wondering if he is going to tell me night travel is prohibited in these areas. But he bends closer and asks me, almost in a whisper, whether I would give him a ride up to Srinagar. I am a little surprised. Why would an army officer want a lift in a civilian taxi when the valley is crawling with the olive-green vehicles of the Indian Army? I hesitate a moment, but then my extroverted self asserts itself. It would be good to have company on this lonely winding mountain road, especially when Ashraf seems to be sulking. I smile and invite him to join me. He asks me to wait a few minutes while he goes to fetch his luggage.

He comes back in civilian clothes and has a small duffel bag with him. He dumps his bag in the boot and gets into the front seat next to Ashraf. Soon, we are off driving into the silent mountains. The Pir Panjal range in the distance is silhouetted against a rising full moon. It is an indescribably beautiful night—serene, silent and stunning in the glow of moonlight. Ours is the only vehicle on this forlorn route.

People who know me think I am gregarious, friendly and perhaps a tad too talkative. Having trekked almost silently for the past three days, I am happy to have someone to converse with, that too in English, since my Hindi is limited, and Urdu non-existent. The handsome young major seems fair game to throw my questions at. When I ask him his name, he mumbles, 'C.' As to his regiment, he is silent. In fact, he seems reluctant to engage in conversation. He answers my persistent questions in monosyllables. Yet he and Ashraf are carrying on a conversation sotto voce. I am truly pissed. After all, I have given this major a lift in my taxi and he doesn't even have the courtesy to answer my questions. May be the arrogance of his rank, I think to myself, as it is now my turn to sulk.

As we drive deeper into the mountains, I notice two things. First, we don't see a single vehicle in either direction except our own. Second, the major is leaning out of the window, intently looking at the road. I wonder what interests them so much on this lonely stretch where the trees throw eerie shadows and the moon sends spangles through the chinks in the tall chinar trees. Are they watching out for a leopard or something? For the next two hours, we drive in uncomfortable silence, while Ashraf veers left and right, a tad unnecessarily, if you ask me.

Suddenly I hear the rumbling of a distant vehicle. A few minutes later, a funny-looking, wide van, unlike anything I have seen before, passes our car. The driver of the van rolls down his window and has a brief conversation with the major and we move on. I strain my ears to listen, but they are talking in whispers.

All of a sudden, both Ashraf and C seem relieved. They heave a sigh of relief, literally, although I have always considered this expression fatuous. They are no longer looking intently at the road, but lean back and visibly relax. I realize it had to do with that vehicle we just passed. I can't contain my curiosity. I ask the major about it. After a brief silence, Major C turns to me and says, 'It is a minesweeper.' The dimwit that I am, I don't first catch the significance of this revelation. It is only after a few minutes that it dawns on me that they both feared this road might have been mined by the militants. Now that the minesweeper has passed us from the opposite direction, it has cleared the road ahead and it is now safe for us to drive on.

Back then, militancy was just beginning in the Valley after decades of peace. Amarnath yatris were sitting ducks. And still are. Which is why there are so many metal detectors and a huge army presence on the yatra route. Embarrassment envelops me. I should have heeded Ashraf's advice and stayed back in Baltal. How is it that I, an educated woman and a journalist to boot, did not realize it would be dangerous to travel at night in the Valley in these times?

Farther down the road, there are quite a few roadblocks and barricades, but we are always waved through because Major C flashes his ID everywhere. From snatches of conversation I have overheard, I gather some militants have been holed up in the mountains and the army has been trying to flush them out. We also see some houses aflame on one of the slopes. Later I learn that militants had burnt down the house of a family they had taken hostage. Around midnight, after many diversions, we reach Srinagar. Major C peels off in some obscure lane while Ashraf drops me off at my hotel. This is one of the eeriest journeys I have ever undertaken, or at least so I think, not knowing what lies in store for me the next day. I mumble an apology to Ashraf and tell him I need to go to the airport early the next day. Surly Ashraf just nods and leaves.

The next morning, after breakfast, I pack my bags and am ready to try my luck at the airport. There are two Air India flights that day and I should be able to get on one. The same white Ambassador arrives, but is driven by a young man. Aziz, Ashraf's son, has come to pick me up. He is a jolly, chatty and somewhat reckless driver. *'Aapko kuch tamasha dhikaoon?'* he asks. I tell him I need to be at the airport early to catch any cancellations that day. But he assures me there's enough time and, anyway, flights to Srinagar are usually late. He weaves in and out of Srinagar roads. At some point, as we are entering a lane, he asks me to crouch under the seat. It seems to be a lonely stretch.

After the previous night's experience, I don't bother to ask any questions, but comply. I fit my bulk into the narrow space between the seats and just peer through the lower part of the window.

Aziz is driving like a maniac, zigzagging through the road. At some point, I hear shots from the right, from one of those deserted houses. The shot misses the car as Aziz drives in a crooked fashion, presumably trying to dodge the bullets. There's more machine-gun firing and one bullet grazes the fender, but Aziz is speeding desperately. I fear we will die of car crash even if the bullets don't get us. And all the while he is laughing like a crazed idiot, which makes me think terror gives him a high. Mercifully, we are soon out of range of the bullets. At the end of this road, which is probably no more than 800 metres, the army has set up a roadblock and cordoned it off too. A huge crowd of uniformed men is gathered on the far end of the road. Aziz stops the car before the barricade and gets down to talk to the jawans who move the barricade to make way for us. As I step out of the car, two officers come towards us. They reprimand Aziz for being so reckless and putting my life in danger as well. The three of us walk side by side and the crowd of jawans splits to let us pass.

It is then I see them—three dead bodies piled on the ground. Three militants—two of them barely out of their teens and a third, perhaps in his forties—had been gunned down by the army, but more are holed up in the deserted house on the road through which Aziz has just taken me.

Aziz knew they were there and had deliberately chosen this road just for the thrill. We stand beside the dead bodies and take our pictures. My encounter with terrorists—to be preserved for posterity.

At the airport, I meet Major C again, and I am eager to share my experience of the morning with him, but he seems impatient to get away from me. I ask him his surname, but he pretends not to hear and moves away. We both are on the same flight, but he avoids me studiously and dissolves into the crowd when we reach Delhi airport. I am disappointed, but over time, life takes over. Major C recedes into the recesses of my memory.

Now I ask him why, long years ago, in the Kashmir Valley, he took a ride with a civilian at night when he had the army vehicle at his disposal. 'Sudha, how do you think I survived in the Valley for seven years through the thick of militancy? I never travelled in army vehicles, never disclosed my Kashmiri surname to anyone, and kept a low profile.'

Annapurna, donning her golden crown for a brief moment every morning

Tangled but not tamed—Kali Gandaki in Mustang

Sphinx and Khufu, a winsome pair

Gaze of the gods—Ramesses II and
Nefertari at Abu Simbel

Reaching out to the sky—minarets of
Jame Mosque in Yazd

Badgirs—air-conditioning, Persian style

Graffiti-lined road to beleaguered Ramallah

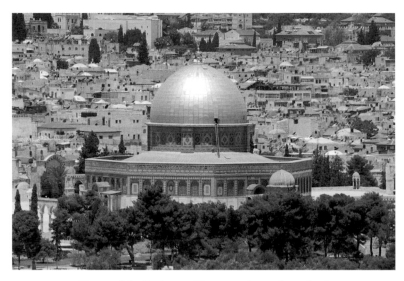

Dome of the Rock—cocking a snook over Jerusalem?

Orthodox Church—a slice of Russia in Jerusalem

Majestic Dome of the Rock—octagon, not square

Sunrise ahoy, on the Irrawaddy

Burmese breakfast bearers wading through the Irrawaddy

Gilt and green—Royal Palace Gardens in Phnom Penh

Khmer gore

Dazzling murals of Luang Prabang

Umbrellas to show off, not shield—night market in Luang Prabang

Islamic architecture, steppe style—Kazan Mosque

Fifty shades of green—Borneo's impenetrable jungles

Buttress roots, haven for creepy crawlies—a creek in the jungles of Borneo

Mix and match—nature's palette, Borneo

The inscrutable Sichuan Buddha

Tea time in the rocky desert of Petra

Artisanal rope bridge across the Siang

Balancing on a rope bridge, a form of meditation, Yingkiong

Fergana's fabled ceramics

A bored lioness in the Serengeti

Always on the alert—Thomson's gazelles, Serengeti

Toasting in Toledo

In 2007, it was still early days. There was no Trivago or TripAdvisor back then. Having blundered through several destinations as a backpacker, I was confident I could enlist the Internet to manage all bookings for our month-long trip through Spain, Portugal and Morocco. R, my friend and travel companion on this trip, bowed to my perceived superior wisdom and let me handle the entire itinerary. It was thus we found ourselves at the Plaza de Zocodover, Toledo's splendid city square, on the hottest day of the year. The plaza itself was impressive, and the fortress perched on the hilltop magnificently sepia-tinted and venerable. The town was somewhere in-between.

Craning our necks to locate our destination for the day, we braced ourselves for the climb up very narrow, very winding and very cobbled streets, crowded with camera-toting tourists and annoyed resident cyclists. Not only did we have to heave ourselves up, but also lug our suitcases stuffed with clothes to last us a month and weighing a ton. After a few minutes of tugging away like a mischievous dog on a leash, the wheels of my suitcase turned recalcitrant; after all, they were designed for the polished floors of airports, not medieval cobbles. Promptly, one broke loose and committed suicide, hurling itself over the cliff. Even as I manoeuvred the disabled luggage with some unsightly acrobatics up the steep hill, the handle pulled ominously to one side, threatening to come off. This was going to take time.

'Eureka!' shouted R, pointing to a signboard which said Santo Tomé—that indeed was the name of our hotel. We huffed and puffed some more and dragged ourselves along, secure in the knowledge that we were almost there. When we finally got up there, the board seemed to be that of a patisserie. We plodded on. The next Santo Tomé was a *churreria* selling churros, a sort of tasteless Spanish pretzel. The third Santo Tomé was a souvenir shop selling picture postcards and keychains to suckers like us, and the fourth a street cafe. And the next one, to be sure, was the church itself, which must have bewitched or browbeaten every business establishment in its extended vicinity, including our budget hotel, to adopt its name.

Cursing the Toledanos for their lack of imagination, I stopped to fish out the map from the cavernous depths of my handbag where I had shoved it. It was only when

I opened it that I realized I had picked up the Spanish version. And to add to my agony, the print was so tiny that I had to grope for my spectacles as well. Clutching the map in one hand and dragging the mangled suitcase with the other, I plodded on some more, ignoring several other Santo Tomés until we finally chanced upon the real one, our budget pad for the next two nights.

It was a family-run place in an old Spanish mansion, with a shop on the ground floor and the reception on the first. I told R to wait on the ground floor and skipped up the carpeted staircase unencumbered by luggage. The receptionist cheerfully informed me our room was on the fourth floor. As I was about to object, she assured me, with a syrupy smile, that it had great views of all of Toledo and was indeed the most sought-after room in the hotel. Or at least that's what I understood, from my limited acquaintance with Spanish-accented English.

Too exhausted to argue, I snatched the keys and ran down the stairs. We somehow managed to hoist both our suitcases up to the elevator opposite the reception. It was only then we realized that this elevator began on the first floor and ended on the third, whereas our room was on the fourth! Before I could turn to ask the receptionist, she had vanished without a trace.

If you think this was sheer bad luck, wait until you see the elevator, which, like Toledo, was a heritage contraption. It had collapsible iron gates, but that was not the problem. It was so tiny that it could ferry either one human or two suitcases at a time. This is what you should expect when a family home metamorphoses into a hotel and even has the temerity to present itself on the World Wide Web as a luxurious hotel at budget prices. I reminded myself of that childhood fable—how an ingenious boatman ferries a tiger, a goat and a bundle of grass intact across the river—for inspiration. After several permutations and combinations and a lot more cursing, we managed to reach our room with our luggage!

Zocodover was like any other European plaza—a cobbled square abutted by cafes and teeming with tourists. It's not hard to imagine that this used to be an Arab souk dealing in livestock trade. The name Zocodover is a corruption of *Souq-al-dawab*, or livestock market. It had seen worse than tourists and livestock though—burnings at the stake, for instance, during the Inquisition, and bullfights too. We wandered around aimlessly and ate marzipan, the typical almond pastry that is a specialty of the town.

Having forgotten the trauma of lugging our suitcase uphill, we jauntily walked around the plaza and spotted a huge queue in front of counter. We joined the line of tourists and bought ourselves tickets to the toy train that would give us a city tour. Blithely we had assumed it would be an air-conditioned coach, which would enthral us with rectangular frames of Toledo from the cool comfort of our seats. But instead, when the Zocotren did arrive, it was a string of open tin boxes—very decorative, no doubt—that had already reached melting point, thanks to its many peregrinations through the streets of Toledo that day. Even as our backsides were toasted by the unpadded tin seats, hot winds blowing from the valley attended to the torso and face. At the end of the journey, we resembled broiled chicken and were none the wiser about the orientation of the city.

The next morning, we stumbled towards that beacon, the Alcázar (*al-qasr* in Arab, meaning the castle), which dominates the Toledo skyline with its four majestic turrets. It has gone through a confusing array of conversions— first built by a Moorish monarch, then repurposed by the Christians as a palace, to be further repurposed into a military garrison and finally left alone to mellow into a gloriously sepia-tinted ruin which can be ticketed to tourists. Unlike the window of our fourth floor room in the hotel, the ramparts of the old Arab city wall give you great view of the pink rooftops of Toledo.

Toledo is an El Greco city. But Toledanos remember their other illustrious compatriot better. Castille La Mancha and Don Quixotes of all sizes stare at you from virtually every shop window. Indeed, you have to be a bit quixotic to include Toledo in your itinerary—something we learnt the hard way on this trip.

2012

Borneo: Raw, Rough and Ravishing

If you believe the rainforest is a tranquil sanctuary to escape to from the tiresome chaos of cities, it's time to question your beliefs! It is a sanctuary, no doubt, just not for you— but for the living, throbbing natural life that tests your survival skills. If the swampy ground doesn't swallow you whole, the venomous insects swarming underfoot will get you, the incessant rain their ready accomplice.

Blissfully unaware of all this, we, a motley group of five Indians, land up in western Borneo, better known as Kalimantan Barat, the ultimate rainforest and the last frontier in biodiversity on planet Earth. We picked Indonesian Borneo over Malaysian Sarawak since it is raw wilderness, not the tourist trap that Sarawak is. We choose Gunung Palung National Park in west Kalimantan to spend a week. Lubuk Baji was to be our pit stop from where we had to explore the jungle. Sure enough, it was not on anyone's map and most certainly not on GPS. You have to be both crazy and hardy to venture into this dreaded outpost.

All of us are crazy enough, but two of us on the verge of senior citizenship discover to our dismay that we are no longer hardy enough. It took us three full days to reach the pit stop. Glenn, our Australian guide, who is more local than the native Dayaks, assures us that more people have attempted scaling Mount Everest than venturing into this part of Borneo.

Unknown to the world, we may have been setting a record of being the first Indians to set foot on this virgin jungle. I had identified this spot after quite a bit of research and had carried on a protracted correspondence with a Dutch adventure enthusiast on *Lonely Planet*'s Thorn Tree forum to identify places where we had a chance of seeing orangutans in the wild. They are shy creatures and difficult to spot. Of course, there are many conservation centres where you can even cuddle one, but we were after the real thing, the wild old man of the forest. West Kalimantan is one of the last refuges of this shy primate. Further surfing helped me locate Glen, an Australian living in Kuching, whom I hired as our guide for this adventure. Arranging stuff through the Internet may appear easy, but throws up unexpected—and perilous—surprises. Glen's hearing was severely impaired, something we discovered only on meeting him face-to-face in Kalimantan. Not much of a help when tramping through a noisy jungle, as we were to find out.

As our travel plans begin to take shape, we realize how remote this place is. It calls for five modes of transport—plane, ferry, SUV, canoe and trek on foot—to reach the jungle. We flew from Delhi to Jakarta and boarded the Air Batavia flight to Pontianak, a town located on the equator in Kalimantan island, also known as Borneo. As the plane crossed the South China Sea and floated over the island, all you could see for almost half an hour was just an endless stretch of oil palm plantations. Stretches of jungles that still remained belched out smoke every few miles. The locals were burning down more forests to grow more oil palms.

Where is the jungle we are headed to? I wonder. Our steward, a young Javanese lad, cannot fathom why this odd bunch would go to Pontianak of all places when there are gorgeous temples in Borobudur and exquisite beaches in Bali. No, he has not heard of Lubuk Baji or Ketapang.

No prizes for guessing what sustains the economy of Pontianak. It is an out-and-out oil town—palm oil, not petroleum. Millions of barrels of this viscous fat are loaded daily on to ships and sent to all parts of the world in the service of cholesterol with a little help from multinationals who boil it in gargantuan vats to process everything from cookies to cakes, pastries, chocolates, frozen desserts, chips, fries and all that junk food we so relish.

Pontianak is also a timber town where zillions of logs clog up the estuaries. We can't resist the temptation to visit the equator monument and take our regulation photographs straddling the two hemispheres across a faint metallic line at its base before we return to our hotel, a seedy rundown establishment that reminds me of Russian hotels in Soviet times. A raucous wedding celebration is under way in the hotel, and we, the only foreigners around, are heartily invited. We take our pictures with the bride and the groom and the rest of the guests, gorge on the hearty feast and return to our gloomy rooms.

The next day we head to the ferry terminal to catch the speedboat to Ketapang, a biggish village, seven sailing hours away. The scene that stares at us at the Pontianak ferry terminal makes us want to rush back to the hotel, which now seems like a pleasure palace compared to this chaos. The terminal is overflowing with humanity, sacks, bags, suitcases and cartons bursting with merchandise; a parade of two-wheelers has already been loaded on the deck with another line waiting to be loaded. Women, kids, families, traders with packages, all are scrambling over each other to claim their six inches of space on the boat. There is only a weekly service to Ketapang.

Glen eyes us warily, wondering if we are up to the task of clambering over luggage and limbs into this overcrowded ferry. Poor Glen, he has never dealt with Indians before and does not know their capacity to plough through any crowds. Adroitly we march towards the jetty, hang on to the railing, trip over luggage, knock kids off balance, upset baskets of poultry and manage to access the gangplank.

There are two decks—both hermetically sealed on all sides and packed with rows of seats covered in outrageously stuffy and smelly upholstery.

Mercifully, every seat is already taken. Every inch of free space on the aisle and corners is also taken up with plastic stools, all occupied. A TV belts out pop music in Bahasa. As we gape in dismay, an usher sheepishly herds us to the farthest corner and offers us plastic stools too. The boat must have at least twice the number of passengers it is allowed to carry.

Soon, the engine lets out a shattering hoot and we are on our way. The passengers have begun unwrapping their breakfast bought at the boat terminal from itinerant vendors, mostly liquids in polythene bags with stuff floating in them. And thus begins the olfactory assault, an unfamiliar aroma so overpowering that I choke even today when I remember it. The floor is turning slippery with liquids dripping from the polythene carry bags. Soon, hundreds of roaches crawl out of the upholstery, eager to get their share.

As the roaches start tickling our toes and the stench becomes unbearable, I wiggle my way through the crowds to push open a door and barge into the captain's cabin. My team follows suit. Being the only foreigners on the boat, we're not shooed off. We flash our most ingratiating smiles and pick our way through the six men lounging around in their sarongs or jeans—no smart white sailors' uniforms here; it's Kalimantan, after all—and plonk ourselves on packages and cartons strewn all over the tiny cabin. It is thick with cigarette smoke. Oh no, we're not complaining about tobacco smell; we are truly grateful that this tobacco smell has effectively masked the smell of food wafting in from the passenger decks. We lean across the window and let the breeze resuscitate our tortured olfactory nerves. A dream landscape with lush mangroves on either bank unfolds. All travails are soon forgotten.

When we reach Ketapang after seven hours, we are greeted by a torrential downpour. Off-loading all the passengers and identifying their assorted luggage takes hours. Glenn has managed an SUV in this outpost and a local Bahasa-speaking guide to boot! Off we go teetering on traces of roads towards the village of Sukadana on the edge of the forest, three hours' drive away.

Sukadana is a neat little village with a high street consisting mostly of eateries with live specimens waiting to be chosen for lunch or dinner. And also a fashion store that has more mannequins than dresses to sell, so much so, some of them are left stark naked. In the produce market, durians announce their presence, miles away. We stay in the only hotel in town, a lovely traditional building with Dayak thatch and a surrounding moat on the edge of the bay. A low tide in the morning reveals a mesmerizing courtship dance of mudskippers of which there are hundreds trapped in the moat, not to mention a couple of water snakes.

Glenn procures our forest permits at Sukadana and we set off the next day into the jungles with Dar, our guide, and Ali, our porter-cum-cook. First we drive for an hour and park our vehicle at the edge of the rainforest. Armed with cameras, tripods, clothes, rainwear, medicines and balms, spare shoes, mosquito netting, bed sheets, etc., each of us is backpacking at least 10 kg. Ali carries the groceries and veggies we purchased from Sukadana. We even have some aromatic Indonesian dark coffee.

We hop on to a small boat which glides gracefully through the Kapuas River and deposits us on the banks near one of the many creeks that radiate from the river. Here, we board two canoes rowed by local boys.

Two young Bornean lads steering our canoe through a dense chlorophyll canopy

We glide through the reddish waters barely visible for the low-hanging canopy. We spy a couple of snakes dangling from the branches and the boat boys deftly manoeuvre the canoe to avoid them. Proboscis monkeys perch on the higher branches. A bird suddenly takes off with a raucous cry as the canoe approaches. We meander through the creek for an hour before we are dropped off on a marshy patch to begin our trek.

This trek is perhaps the most difficult I have undertaken in all my travels. The terrain is a soggy swamp of sodden leaves, at least a metre high. Your foot sinks up to your ankles as you step on the ground. The jungle begins on a steep slope strewn with moss-covered boulders that dodge the crampons in your trekking boots to dislodge you. Felled tree trunks sprouting fluorescent toadstools advertise poison as they block your path challenging you to an obstacle race. Torrential rains have churned the mud into a slushy trap, underneath which lurk creatures unseen. What we do see is enough to give us the creeps—6-inch-long, finger-thick centipedes and glowing red millipedes crawl everywhere, giant leeches, fat snails, and armies of other insects whose names I don't know swarm underfoot. I have a stick to help me gauge the terrain, but very often, I have to cling to the vines and trunks to keep myself from tripping or slipping and when I do that, bright red killer ants crawl up my limbs and under my clothes. In many places, Glenn throws us a rope secured to a tree trunk to which we cling to be hoisted up inch by painful inch. The rainforest trek is particularly challenging for the bespectacled. You're forever wiping the water off your glasses, and even when the rain stops, it is so steamy that you can hardly see where you're going anyway.

For seven hours we trudge through pristine and primordial jungle, stopping every now and then to catch our breath. The trees are disdainfully tall, reaching out to the skies. The canopy is so dense that the sky is visible only in coin-sized chinks that let in light rather reluctantly. Humidity hangs heavy and mosquitoes buzz annoyingly. We are often distracted by the antics of the simians on treetops, but unless you watch your every step, you could land on the forest floor and end up as feedstock for the steamy compost in the making. So, practically, you miss the wood for the next step; forget about taking out your camera, fixing the lens and shooting the orangutans and their aerial acrobatics. Anyway, they are so high on the canopy that even my 400-mm lens will produce only a blur. For the present, each of us is focused on just one goal—reaching that elusive shelter which, I am sure, has been conjured up by Dar's hallucinations. Who would have gone and built a shelter in this jungle?

Dar is an experienced guide, although our group is probably the least fit that he has ever guided. He cajoles and scolds, and leads us farther and farther into jungle towards that mythical shelter. Sceptical and murderous, we follow him for want of a better option. The rain now falls in thick sheets with a roar and all our gear including camera bag and passport pouch are dripping ominously. M and my son K, both teenagers, sprint like springboks, while

SJ and I limp behind, cursing ourselves for undertaking this foolhardy venture. B brings up the rear, slipping in the mud, staggering over boulders and too traumatized to even curse or scold.

And suddenly we hear human voices floating through the foliage. We are sure our imagination is playing tricks. But then, we come across two tents on the forest floor on the banks of a creek where three young boys are engaged in typical camping chores. One is filling up water from the creek in a plastic bottle while the other is trying to light a fire, presumably, to cook the meal. We are tempted to collapse in this haven of civilization, but Dar cracks the whip and makes us plod on.

After about ten minutes of this struggle, we finally spot the shed that had so tantalized us. We screech like sailors sighting land after months. With two giant strides, B crosses the stream and goes and sprawls on a fallen tree-trunk so narrow that it can only hold a third of his girth. And in a jiffy, he is snoring even as a spider and a few ants crawl over his trousers; that he manages to slumber in this precarious position for the next three hours is testament to the extent of his exhaustion. No eiderdown and mattress could have achieved the level of comfort or induced such repose.

All through our stay in Lubuk Baji, Ali was our lifesaver, literally. He would fetch firewood, improvise a stove with rocks, coax the damp wood to light up and produce hot meals fit for kings—noodles, rice, vegetables, all topped up with aromatic black coffee. No Michelin-star restaurant could have rustled up a more delectable repast, no resort conjured up such a gorgeous setting. This was raw nature. Nothing could rival it.

The next few days are spent foraying out of this precarious shelter to check out the rainforest and retreating into it at night. With just four wooden pillars supporting a roof and no walls, Lubuk Baji conspires with the elements, giving them free passage, as we shiver on the naked wooden floor all night. Those few days are enough to make us realize the rainforest is as cacophonous as peak-hour traffic at the ITO crossing in Delhi. By day, the gibbons and macaques swing violently from branch to branch, settling scores over territory. An orangutan mum hops across the canopy,

Buttress roots and bromeliads lining the creek feeding into the Kapuas River in Borneo

violently snapping branches and grunting loudly to scare intruders. If it is fruiting season, the avians will join the simians in the brawl over choice pickings of stinky durian. Hornbills join the cacophony with their rotor-like wings whirring like a helicopter. All these sounds are eclipsed by the roar of the rain that never stops, accompanied by thunder for percussion.

By night, it is a different world altogether. Even as the birds retire for the day, insects of all digits and denominations, as vain as they are venomous, crawl out of the woodwork (literally) to begin their choral symphony. Some flaunt their fluorescence while most announce their presence through their vocal chords. One mimics a sawmill in action, another strums a tuneful drone that would put the latest caller tune on your cell phone to shame, a third shatters your eardrums with its searing cry—not unlike the tile-cutting machine that harries you in urban jungles under construction. The cicadas set up their background screech while a dozen frogs croak lustily, their libidos tickled by the incessant downpour. You can't see them, unless you risk venturing into the forest floor in the dark, but it is not difficult to imagine how puffed up the male must be, his translucent skin stretched taut on his tense body as he calls out to his mate.

The rainforest seeps into every cell of our body during these days. But it does more than that, as I soon find out. On one of my excruciating trips to the loo, I find my lingerie is bloody; in fact, blood is trickling down my thigh although I feel no pain. I panic, thinking I have hurt my innards. After some investigation, I prise away a couple of leeches from my nether regions. How they got all the way in there is still a mystery to me.

Even now, years later, I sometimes wake up in the middle of a nightmare, hands flailing to prise out the obstinate leeches, the rainforest having seeped into my psyche as well. Yet, not for a moment do I regret the surreal days we spent in the jungle, days in which we glimpsed something precious, intimate and unique. I would go again, if I could.

2000

Frozen in Norwegian Summer

The automatic currency-changing machine at Oslo Central does not like my dollar bill. It spits it out every time I feed it into the slot. I try various denominations, but without any success. It is a Sunday evening and the adjacent forex counter had just closed. I need Norwegian kronors for the tram ride to my hotel about 5 km away.

Earlier in the evening, as soon as I arrived from Stockholm, I had offloaded my luggage at one of those yawning lockers to take an unencumbered stroll around the town while there was still daylight. Now I need a 20 Norwegian kronor coin to retrieve my suitcase. I am stuck, and outside there is steady rain. It is also getting dark. I curse the machine, which I suspect of being racist; otherwise, why should it spit out my perfectly legal greenbacks? After a few more attempts, I give up and head into the streets.

I go out in the sleet to Karl Johans Gate (the Swedish *gata* had become the Norwegian Gate), the high street in Oslo. The street stretches for about a mile with glittering shops on both sides enticing you to buy, buy and buy. I look for forex counters, of which there are four, but each one of them is closed. There are ATMs every few yards, but unfortunately, I have not memorized my secret code for drawing cash; it is scrawled on a piece of paper safely locked up in my suitcase, which in turn is safely stuck in the station locker. I decide to do without it.

Tram number five trundles to a halt in front of me and I stroll in confidently and pull my cap over my forehead and, without a word, push my Swedish krona into the tray. The lady driver doubling as conductor asks me something in Norwegian and I just nod my head. The machine rumbles and spits out a ticket. I hastily pull it out and saunter down the aisle and park myself in front of an old lady with loads of shopping. I nervously keep glancing at the driver through the rear-view mirror hanging in front of her, but she's oblivious of my existence, leave alone my minor misdemeanour.

The tram drops me ten stops away—which is where the hotel brochure had asked me to get off. The rain has turned the thawing snow into ugly slush. A long, slippery road stretches ahead of me. I gingerly press my shoe into the ice and it goes right in. In a moment, my toes tingle—through five layers of socks. My throat is parched and the snow makes me disoriented. Every house looks the same and there's not a soul on the street.

I trudge patiently, trying to read the map in the brochure. After a good twenty-minute walk—about which the brochure had not warned me—I stumble into the hotel, bedraggled but relieved. At least I have my passport and my handbag with me. Tomorrow morning I have to catch the train to Bergen to take the famous Flåm Railway for which I have already bought tickets and a ScanRail pass.

The narrow strip of the Norwegian coast forms the back of the tiger, which marks the map of Scandinavia. It's a craggy coast with deep inlets and some spectacular fjords. Everyone, including my *Lonely Planet* guide, had advised me to take the multimodal journey through the fjords if I wanted to get a taste of Norway in a nutshell. Since I have only three days in Norway, I decide to give Oslo the royal miss and head straight to Bergen from where the fjord trip begins. Early morning, I set out from my hotel after changing a hundred-dollar bill at the counter at a terribly discounted rate and head for the railway station for the famous Flåm Rail trip. It is a combination of train, boat and bus rides to see the fjords.

The seven-hour train ride to Bergen, past forests, alpine villages and the starkly beautiful Hardangervidda Plateau, is followed by a ferry ride up the spectacular Nærøyfjord to Gudvangen, a bus ride to Voss and a train back to Bergen.

The train is virtually empty and I have the luxury of almost an entire compartment to myself. Frame after rectangular frame of Norwegian countryside fleets past with wooden cottages that look straight out of a Christmas card.

I almost expect to see Santa Claus and his reindeer chariot parked near one of those red-brick chimneys. Except that it's not December, but April. Yet, the temperature outside is in the minus and this is all-year-round ski country through which I am travelling.

At Geilo, one of the midway stations, you can step out of the train straight into a cable car which will lift you up to the ski slopes. When the train stops at Geilo, my suzerainty over the compartment is at an end. The coach is invaded by hordes of modern-day Vikings with longish skis that look as deadly as the Viking spears. In a moment, they have come and colonized my compartment, dumping their luggage everywhere and hanging their fluorescent-coloured jackets and windcheaters from the pegs.

The Flåm train is actually a toy affair. It has just two compartments and exactly eight passengers. In fact, I am impressed that there are seven other fools like me, wide-eyed about snow. The train wends its way through the mist to begin its steep descent into the Flåm valley. I feel I am in an aircraft because nothing is visible out of the window. The glossy brochure never mentioned this possibility. There, all the pictures are in rainbow colours and vividly clear. I lurch from side to side as the train takes its twists and turns and seems to plunge into the valley. After a couple of hours, we reach Flåm, where a wooden railway compartment doubles as a restaurant.

The boat for Gudvangen will not sail for another couple of hours, and I have enough time to stroll around Flåm.

I take a walk around the town and find that many houses have rooms to let and there's even a youth hostel bang in the middle of the town. So bad their business today seems to be, they would have gladly rented their rooms to me, a youth in her late forties. Flam is a one-horse town with a single shop, single railway station and a single restaurant catering solely to tourists.

The motorboat takes off finally, shattering the calm of the fjords. Once again, visibility is near zero and all I can see is the foamy trail left in the wake of the boat. The brochures had promised bushes full of strawberries so close that you could reach out and help yourself. They had carried pictures of picnicking families on a magnificently flat fjord—as if someone had neatly sliced the top off the hill—of which I see no sign now. I learn we are traversing the Nærøyfjord, the most magnificent of all Norwegian fjords, only when the captain announces this.

The bus journey to a rain-washed Voss takes me on the other side of the Sognefjord, the longest and deepest of the Norwegian fjords. A frozen stream accompanies us all the way, but I spy some tantalizing glimpses of the deep blue water from time to time. The route is picture-postcard perfect—in fact, I might have been better off gazing at the picture postcard than freezing here in this monochrome landscape.

2014

Stuck with the Buddha in Sichuan

Sichuan seldom figures on the global tourist itinerary. Eclipsed by seductive Shanghai, intimidating Beijing and, increasingly, historic Xian, this province seems content to remain in the shadows. Some of the travelling pack—mostly Chinese domestic tourists—stray into Chengdu, the capital of Sichuan, primarily to glimpse and cuddle that black-and-white furball endemic to this region.

But a visit to the Giant Panda Breeding Station in Chengdu disabuses you of your notions about the adorable-looking bear. Try cuddling the animal and you will get a bleeding gash on your face and a solid kick too, before it wriggles out of your hold and crushes your toe in the process. The animal is neither cuddly nor friendly. Like all wild animals, it recoils from touch, and you need to keep your distance, which the research station is at pains to drill into you, often in vain. If you're that keen on a cuddle for your Instagram, cough up a hefty fee to hold a domesticated panda that poses like a pro in the presence of the paparazzi.

Unsurprisingly, many tourists do pay to cuddle, in this land where the selfie is a national obsession even more than in India, and the panda a national icon. A few even volunteer to pick up panda poo and sweep the enclosures for the privilege of being on the inside of the fence. My friend and I do neither, but just saunter through the research station ogling through the fence at pandas of various age groups putting up virtuoso performances. One is hanging upside down, another busy chewing bamboo, a third sits like a human, hind legs outstretched, playing with a stick.

IV and I are in Sichuan for an entirely different purpose. RB, my friend and fellow traveller on a different journey, had piqued my curiosity about a big and beautiful Maitreya Buddha carved out of an entire mountainside in Sichuan. In fact, some history books claim Mount Emei was where Buddhism was first established in China, during the Tang dynasty; the Leshan Buddha is the world's tallest pre-modern statue. Mount Emei has been accorded the UNESCO World Heritage Site tag, although that means little when the title is distributed like pizza fliers to all and sundry.

We had arrived in Chengdu the previous day, by the fancy high-speed, high-tech train, all the way from Lhasa where we had spent the previous week. On the train, soft seat compartments pamper you with your own TV screen like in an aircraft, a pair of slippers, unlimited supply of steaming hot water, and oxygen masks if you need them at those altitudes through which the train cruises. But no one seems to turn on the TV, what with the scenery outside being so stunning. Everyone gets off the train at Tanggula station to take their regulation photographs. At 16,627 feet, it is the highest railway station in the world, trumping Cusco in Peru by more than 5000 feet.

Chengdu is an indistinguishable modern Chinese city mauled by malls and minted fashion designers. We have neither the money nor the inclination to savour its many delights, and hence look for a way to get to Mount Emei directly. The picturesque town of Leshan, the springboard for Mount Emei, is about five hours away by road. Not familiar with the language or the terrain, we opt for a tour bus, which would take us there and bring us back after a couple of days.

Early next morning, when we arrive at the boarding point for the bus tour, there is bedlam. This is a long weekend in China and virtually everyone and his uncle is heading out somewhere. There are a dozen buses departing for myriad destinations in all directions. There is a sea of humanity milling around the buses. We seem to be the lone non-Chinese. How do we locate our bus in this crowd? After much miming and clowning, we eventually reach it.

The tour guide in our bus is a portly Chinese, but that's not the problem; he is hopelessly unilingual, and the Chinese tourists annoyingly garrulous. Not only won't we be learning much about the history of the place on this tour, we would be missing out on much more—as we find out. Over the next three days, while everyone else gorges on platefuls of everything that creeps, crawls, slithers, grunts and squeals, IV and I, the only vegetarians in the group, gulp down blanched beans meal after meal. The resultant flatulence was our sweet revenge on our fellow travellers cackling away throughout the trip.

After five hours on winding and forested roads, the bus deposits us at a shady-looking hotel in Leshan. We find out it is called Traders' Hotel. The lobby is gaudy enough to set alarm bells ringing in our heads. Predictably, the faucets are leaky, the carpets musty, and the flush doesn't work. There is a mild drizzle. We check in, freshen up and start our climb up the steep steps to the fabled Buddha statue. En route, we have to brave dozens of huge pink macaques glistening with raindrops and grinning with glee as they snatch my bag to investigate. They are particularly fond of cell phones and cameras, but fortunately, both are safe in my backpack. A burly macaque expertly opens my water bottle, takes a sip and flings it at me with all the contempt it can muster.

We huff and puff up the meandering steps to the top. We stop at the sprawling Dafo monastery, light incense sticks, and proceed. Just as we turn the bend, the Buddha's smiling visage comes into view. We are awestruck by the sheer scale of this Buddha. Having visited hundreds of Buddhist shrines all over the world, I have seen many huge Buddhas, seated in meditation, standing upright and even reclining when there is not enough vertical space, but the Leshan Buddha trumps all of them. We learn later that it is indeed the world's largest Buddha. Heavy-lidded and with an inscrutable smile, this 71-metre giant watches over the confluence of three rivers—Minjiang, Dadu and Qingyi.

The inscrutable Leshan Buddha

Like all such places, this too has a local legend. During the Tang dynasty—yes, you read that right, not Ming, not Qing, but Tang—in the eighth century, a monk called Hai Tong began carving this giant statue to appease the raging rivers that routinely capsized villagers' boats. Although the carving lasted all of ninety years, longer than Hai Tong's time, the giant Buddha did take care of the problem. Of course, it would. All that debris from the carving was dumped directly into the confluence below, stemming its flow and turning it into a tame and stagnant pool where tourist boats now float listlessly.

Leshan Buddha seems to have a huge crowd of visitors today, most of them fashionable young Chinese. I am impressed at the devotion of the youth who leave glitzy Chengdu and its designer malls to come to this remote mountain to pray to the Buddha. Until I see most of them taking selfies (Chinese always carry a selfie stick with their phones) pretending to hold the Buddha's serene visage between their palms, or posing as if they are pinching his nose or pulling his topknot. Indeed, Leshan Buddha is a star attraction because he offers irresistible photo ops. He puts up with all this, with an unwavering and benign smile.

We meander through the serene hills and visit many monasteries and temples. In the evening, we are herded to a Sichuan opera. Dancers on stage change face masks multiple times, each in the twinkling of an eye. A swish of their arms, a rapid pirouette and, lo and behold, the face of the dancer, which was a fearsome demon a second ago, is now a benign goddess. I try not to blink, but still can't see how they do it. Apparently, this is a Sichuan specialty and a fiercely guarded secret.

Early morning on the third day, we pack our bags and get ready to go back to Chengdu where we have a flight to catch later in the evening. But as we descend to the hotel lobby, we find our fellow bus-mates are sprawled on the sofas and chairs, even spilling on to the carpeted floor. They seem to be in no hurry to board the bus, which should be leaving in minutes. There is no sign of their luggage either. Worse, the lobby is eerily and unusually silent.

Our fellow travellers eye us with interest as we ignore them and head towards the bus. Suddenly a stick emerges from a bush to block our way. Holding it is a wizened old woman. She raises it and shoos me back to the hotel. Behind her, there seems to be some sort of a picket assembled hurriedly with chairs, stools, and whatever else the locals could manage. A dozen odd people, mostly the elderly, are assembled around the picket. The tour bus is parked under a tree beyond the picket.

Emboldened by our foreignness, we brush past the old woman and sprint our way to the bus. A few old men move menacingly towards us, shouting and gesticulating wildly, presumably asking us to go back. The bus door is shut and there's no sign of the driver anywhere. We hastily retreat to the lobby of the hotel where a bemused crowd of smirking faces awaits us. We shuffle uneasily, dump our bags near the reception counter and again head out to watch the tamasha.

In a while, more locals join the picket. Housewives amble in twos and threes, presumably after completing their domestic chores. Women with babies and a few smoking men too stand around idly. More furniture gets piled on. Over the next couple of hours, the crowd swells to a couple of hundreds. It is a motley and somewhat aggressive crowd now. Occasionally, slogans are raised.

Our efforts to find out the reason for this protest draw a blank, for want of linguistic felicity. But I am truly impressed that these people in a remote mountain village are gutsy enough to protest in public and picket in a country that has elevated unquestioning compliance to authority into a national obligation.

A van drives by and stops near the crowd. Out jump six or seven cops, dressed in uniform. I crane my neck to see whether they disperse the crowds—after all, this is China. But they just park themselves under the shade of the trees; some pull out their cigarette packets and light up. Soon, a second and a third van pull up and more policemen jump out. The picketers start shouting slogans and some placards appear out of nowhere.

Hours sail by. The cops look bored, but there is no sign of any attempt at resolution, whatever the problem. Around lunchtime, noodle boxes appear and the picketers turn picnickers. A couple of cops start playing games on their cell phones, perhaps to distract their attention away from the all-pervading aroma of food. IV and I are too anxious to feel the pangs of hunger.

By now, it is late afternoon. I begin to panic. We have to be at Chengdu airport by 10 p.m. to catch our flight back home. If picketing continues for the next couple of hours, we are sure to miss our flight. I look around and pick a senior-looking officer among the cops. His midriff is sufficiently bulging, his hair receding halfway across his skull and his lapel more striped than the rest. I march up to him and tell him we need to go back to Chengdu now or we will miss our flight back home. This, accompanied by miming of a plane taking off. He stares blankly at us and goes back to picking his nose. The protesters eye us with hostility. Even if the cops let us pass, the villagers are not going to, I realize.

Distraught, we retreat to the lobby of the hotel and sulk. A few minutes later, the manager of the hotel waddles towards us with our bags and leads us out the back door. We walk away from the village into a forest. After about 500 yards, we spy a road, and lo and behold, a Mercedes with a police beacon is parked discreetly away from prying eyes. Obviously, the protesters hadn't bargained for wily foreigners and secretive cops making common cause to outwit them. This village road, right under their nose, so to speak, is completely unattended, while the main highway down the mountain is fully barricaded and fortified. The hotel manager deposits our bags in the boot and opens the door for us to get in. We can't believe our luck. The car drives us out of the mountains through country roads and into Chengdu—in just three hours! Surely, the nose-picking cop had something to do with this?

2000

The Playful Ganga Mai

No artist's palette could have reproduced the colour scheme as strikingly. On one side are the emerald mountains— majestic and so steep that they appear to rise almost vertically. On the other, the dazzling white beaches with their fine powdery sand interrupted by stretches of grey rocks of assorted shapes and sizes. Above is a sliver of the cobalt sky. In the middle is the jade ribbon of the Ganga— limp, serene and content. Don't let her fool you though. Beneath the apparent placidity, she conceals a range of dizzying moods—mostly mysterious and contemplative, at times effervescent, and occasionally dangerous and diabolical. She can be the tempestuous Mandakini, the playful Bhagirathi and the impetuous Jahnavi. But at the moment, she seems to have donned her 'Ganga Mai' avatar—calm, benign and reassuring.

Your raft glides effortlessly with the current, swaying ever so gently. Its inflated sides bounce off the waves playfully and you're lulled into believing that it is invincible. After all, you've donned your life jacket and helmet, and were not daydreaming when the river guide barked his instructions. There are ten others in your raft. And a dozen more in the other two that follow yours. There must be some security in numbers?

Even as you begin to enjoy the smoothness of the ride, Riju, your river guide, orders you all to climb on the sides of the raft. You look at him in disbelief and point out that you can't swim. But he's unimpressed and poker-faced as he urges you on. You consider mutiny, but then, he's the boss on the raft and you had agreed to obey his instructions. You had even signed away your rights, indemnifying the rafting company against any claims in the event of a mishap. You realize that your options are rather limited. Reluctantly, you heave yourself up on the slippery rounded sides, link hands with the others to form a chain and try to balance as best as you can. The raft bounces about clumsily on the waves. You lurch and sway dangerously. Riju seems indifferent to your plight as he rows furiously downstream.

And then you hear it before you see it—the roar of the approaching rapids. By the time you figure out the source of the roar, it's too late. Terror immobilizes you as you're sloshed over by the frothy waters of Daniel's Dip, the first of the series of imaginatively named rapids on the Rishikesh stretch of the Ganga. Your knees buckle.

All of you collapse inside the raft, in a tangle of arms and limbs. But you're grateful to be breathing. As you struggle to extricate yourselves, Riju comes to your rescue, but only to push you unceremoniously over the sides of the raft into the swirling waters below. The receding roar of the rapids you just crossed is drowned by shrieks of fright. Your flailing arms miss their hold on the rings attached to the sides of the raft and you think this is it—the end. Your loved ones fleet past your mental screen and you say your last goodbyes.

But then—what's this? Who's pulling you? Some invisible hand seems to be dragging you out of the water. In a moment you're afloat again. Of course you still don't trust the life jacket which is just doing its job of keeping you afloat. As you bob up, you see the impish smile on Riju's face. He tells you to lie on your back and enjoy the float. The water is incredibly chilly and it tickles the back of your neck as it makes its way into the crevices in your helmet. You're too stiff to let go. You abuse and cajole alternately and finally persuade Riju to throw you a rope to which you cling for dear life.

But after a while you realize that you're not going to drown after all. The terror slowly disappears and you soon begin to enjoy the float. By now even your body's thermostat has adjusted itself to the surrounding temperature and you no longer shiver and tremble. You feel light and invincible. The swirling waters are no longer threatening. It feels more like a caress. Time stands still as you bob up and down with the rhythm of the river. The afternoon sun sends out comforting rays of warmth. There is a sense of exhilaration that pervades you. This is life, you say to yourself. Floating on the cool waters and drifting along with the current under the cobalt sky is no less than paradise itself.

The placid stretch of Ganga Mai is but a short one. As the distant roar of 'Wall', the biggest rapid on this course, reaches your ears, the panic returns. Riju heaves you back into the raft one by one and just in time too. This time, you don't stand on the sides, but crowd into the well of the raft and lean towards the stern with your feet tucked securely under the partition. The rubber vessel pitches and lurches dangerously close to the mountainside where it takes a sharp turn. And lo and behold, the next thing you see is a wall of white gushing water that storms into your nose, mouth, face and over your head. This must be it—the *pralayam* that our scriptures warned us about, the deluge that the Bible talked about. Your senses shut down momentarily as you're tossed about like pebbles in a rattle, but you hold on for dear life.

Soon you're again on another placid stretch where you amuse yourselves, throwing buckets of water on each other. This time you don't wait for Riju to order you into the river. To a woman, everyone is out in the water and all the three rafts are empty but for the oarsmen. The banks are dotted with beaches every few yards and there is a neat row of colourful tents in each one of them. Other rafts come into view. There is much shouting and water-throwing. A few kayaks pass by and you tell Riju that you want to try one too. He seems to be in an indulgent mood. He stops a passing kayak, tells the occupant—apparently another river guide—to jump into the water, and holds it for you with a flourish. Very confidently, you slide your sizeable bulk into the narrow space and grin triumphantly. But before you can even strap yourself in place, the kayak overturns and you find yourself in the nether regions of Ganga Mai's belly. She rushes in to check your nose, ears, eyes, mouth, and you gasp for breath and flail your arms helplessly (your poor legs are packed too closely into the kayak). Riju's demonic chuckle sounds ominously far away. You wiggle your legs out of the kayak somehow. A few seconds of this agony and the life jacket reasserts itself to bring you back to the surface.

Some distance later, you have your brush with Ed, the villain of the river. As you float away from the raft, he stalks you from behind and drags you, screaming. You're vertical for a few seconds, and however much you try, you're unable to extricate yourself from his vice-like grip. You're dizzy as he swirls you round and round. This time Riju doesn't laugh, but transforms himself into a knight in shining armour. He and Harish from the other raft swim furiously towards you and drag you by the lapels of your life jacket. In a few seconds, you're back in the safety of the raft, thoroughly chastened by the experience. Your mates mock you about your date with Ed—the vicious eddies that gobble up unsuspecting victims—but the concerned looks on the faces of the river guides tell you that you just had a close shave.

You are taken through a series of rapid-fire rapids. Trust rafting companies to name the rapids evocatively: Rapid Fire, Sweet Sixteen, Crossfire, Return to Sender, Three Blind Mice, Roller Coaster, Golf Course, Double Trouble and even one called Black Money because it happens to be near a cottage built by an industrialist! After the first few, you get the hang of the drill on how to negotiate them. There are five of them that are Grade IV (expedition level), and the others Grade III. At the end of the third day, you've toted up six hours of rapids-rafting in three phases—from Kaudiyala to Marine Drive, from Marine Drive to Shivpuri and from Shivpuri to Rishikesh. That's impressive. You are patted on the back and told that you've been very brave and can now go on to expedition level on the Bhagirathi or Alaknanda run and then on to Kali-Sharda, Beas and even the Brahmaputra!

At that time, little do you realize that the real test of your courage was not the rapids. Later that evening, back at your tent camp on the sandy beach, you savour a hot dinner by the campfire and recount the day's thrills. A full moon floods the valley with luminescent light. Suddenly, you hear a blood-curdling scream from the opposite bank. A white figure in flowing robes seems to float on the mountainside across the river. Even in the light of the full moon, you can barely make out its contours. An eerie silence envelopes the camp which only moments ago was abuzz with merriment. Riju and party whisper some legends about local ghosts to an already terrified audience. All eyes are fixed on the opposite bank, but the figure seems to have vanished. No one seems to be in a hurry to go back to their tents. Perhaps everyone is waiting for someone else to take the lead. Fear hangs, thick and palpable.

Your heart misses a beat when moments later, a kayak pulls up on your beach. Even as you're contemplating dashing up the mountainside and away from the river, out jumps Tarun, one of the camp organizers. As he takes off his life jacket, you notice he's wearing a white shirt. He pulls out a white sheet with a flourish, wraps it loosely around his shoulders and mimics the blood-curdling shriek of the ghost on the other bank. Then he breaks into peals of laughter. He's joined by his colleagues from the camp. You realize that your hosts have spared no effort to give you an absolutely thrilling time.

2010

Worm's-Eye View from Palestine

Riding the elevator to the top of the Eiffel Tower or the chairlift to the Great Wall of China for a stunning bird's-eye view may be on the bucket list of millions of tourists, but we pride ourselves on being travellers, not mere tourists, don't we? Never mind if it calls for a generous dose of masochism. Therefore, we opt for a worm's-eye view, of Ramallah and Biblical Jericho, no less, even if it entails driving through long stretches of barricades, barbed wires and bazooka-toting guards of conflicted neighbours Israel and Palestine.

Kapilan, my teenage son, and I are on an extended visit to Jerusalem and the West Bank in Palestine. After a brief visit to the Church of Nativity at Bethlehem on the Palestinian side, we go in search of a taxi that would take us to Ramallah and Jericho. It so happens we are in Palestine the day after a Turkish flotilla carrying food supplies to Gaza was shot down by Israelis. Scores of Palestinians in black clothes are protesting silently outside the Church of Nativity. The solemnity and gravitas of the protest—just holding up placards without speaking a word—bespeak a sense of dignity that only the long-suffering can muster.

Unlike Israel, Palestine wears a weary, war-torn look. We go looking for transport to Ramallah, the capital. From the look of the place, we expect to get only beat-up jalopies, or worse, donkey carts for taxis. But surprise, surprise, all taxis here are Mercs, no less. Some haggling and we hop into the swanky-looking vehicle and speed off through graffiti-laden, deserted streets. The Merc's windows rattle and refuse to roll up. This Merc is no less beat-up, except, its polished exteriors reveal little of its pathetic health. Of course the air conditioning doesn't work. It must be 42 °C. But Naif is a chatty driver and we feel a sense of kinship with the beleaguered Arabs as he rattles off their myriad woes.

We hurtle down the highway to Ramallah. Barbed wires, barricades, spiked walls, massive gates and uniformed men signal the visitor to keep a safe distance. There are stretches where the wall is reinforced concrete at least two feet thick, draped over with barbed wire and towers with gunmen to boot. The graffiti and posters seem excessive even to the jaded Indian eye. Traffic on the road is thin. You pass an occasional donkey cart.

I wonder aloud why anyone would fight over this wasteland. Kapilan, a history buff, looks at me with all the derision he can muster and reprimands me. 'Do you realize this is the most hallowed piece of real estate on planet Earth?' It is at his insistence we are doing this trip. I sulk silently.

Ramallah looks every bit the beleaguered and besieged capital of Palestine. It is a tiny enclave on the West Bank of the Jordan River—referred to simply as the West Bank, surrounded on three sides by Israel and its now-infamous wall. In fact, the wall cuts right through East Jerusalem, taking livelihood away from thousands of Arabs trapped on the Palestinian side. East Jerusalem is where all the holy sites are: the Temple Mount, the Dome of the Rock, the Wailing Wall and the Church of the Holy Sepulchre. Israel took over this land in the Six-Day War in 1967.

People in the West Bank are trapped as much by their geography as by their politics. Other than the barbed-wire barricade separating them from Israel, the only border they have is with Jordan through what is called the King Hussein Bridge. Palestine, like the erstwhile Pakistan, is in two bits. The other bit is the infamous Gaza Strip, virtually a strip of Mediterranean Coast adjoining Egypt and separated from the West Bank by vast stretches of Israeli territory. The third piece, Golan Heights to the north adjoining Syria, has been occupied and appropriated by Israel since 1967. Palestinians from Ramallah cannot go to Gaza and vice versa, and when they travel abroad, they use the Jordanian airport.

After a few hours, we enter Ramallah, a dusty town with concrete apartment blocks and nary a feature to distinguish itself. We make our way to the single attraction in this derelict town—the tomb of Yasser Arafat. Arafat's smiling visage draped in telltale scarf dominates the government buildings, peeping from rooftops through a tangle of electric wires.

At Arafat's Mausoleum, we surrender our passports to the security. Instant smiles light up their faces as they glance at our passports. Indians are welcome, the officer says deferentially, and escorts us to the tomb to pay our respects to their departed leader. A proud Palestinian flag flutters atop the grave.

We get back into the car and drive to Jericho, a couple of hours away, through more dust-blown, dreary roads. En route, we pass some tombs covered in green and red silken chadors.

Jericho seems to be an oasis in the desert. The town is full of leafy neighbourhoods and sprawling bungalows peeking through a profusion of palm fronds. Jericho sprawls on a flat plain abutted by ruddy-hued hillocks on one side and the grey sliver of the Dead Sea shimmering on the horizon. The infamous West Bank of the Jordan River is no more than a dried-up ditch with nary a drop of water. The settlement is an oasis nourished, no doubt, by many springs and fresh-water sources that are not readily visible. Even in the Bible, Jericho was referred to as the City of Palm Trees.

Old Jericho or the Biblical town is situated on the slopes of the hillock with its warren of caves. You can huff and puff your way up the 1.3-km trekking track to reach the Greek Monastery of the Temptation atop the cliff or you can simply glide up on a cable car for an astronomical fee. With temperatures on the wrong side of 40 °C and one of us on the wrong side of fifty, there is little choice but to cough up the unconscionable fare and ride on the dangling contraption. Just as well—you get spectacular views of dense banana plantations and emerald squares of orange trees.

What they don't tell you at the cable car station though is that the car doesn't ride all the way up. It deposits you midway to the old town and you still have more winding slopes to conquer before you reach the entrance to the cave where Jesus Christ is believed to have fasted for forty days. There are more caves and canyons beyond, but in this heat, all one can do is to escape into the cool and cavernous interiors of the monastery carved into the hillside. It was to this piece of real estate on earth that Joshua, successor to Moses, first led the Israelites when they escaped from bondage in Egypt. The monastery was first constructed in the sixth century CE on the hillock identified as the Mount of Temptation because it was here that Jesus undertook penance to resist the temptations held out by Satan.

Then came the Arabs who overran Palestine and conquered most of these areas including Jericho sometime around 630 CE. The Crusaders came nearly 500 years later to rescue Jericho from the Arabs and built two churches on the slopes. Later, the Arabs reclaimed Jericho from the Christians and demolished these churches. Towards the end of the nineteenth century, the Greek Orthodox Church purchased the land from the Arabs and built this monastery around the cave in which Jesus is believed to have stayed. In the end, like most sacred sites, faith is what determines its provenance.

At this time of the day, we are the lone visitors to the monastery and we're allowed to roam freely around the premises, although warned not to take photographs. The cave is bare and cool. There is a Greek chapel with exquisite frescos of biblical scenes. A stone slab with a cross cut out of its middle hangs from a balcony perched on the cliff side. It offers a tantalizing view of Jericho through the slits.

Jericho never lets you forget it is the oldest continuously inhabited town on the planet, although Damascus in Syria and our own Varanasi also lay claim to the same fame as do many other cities across continents. Archaeological remains unearthed in Jericho point to a settlement as early as 8000 BCE. In later periods too, Jericho seems to have been a hot favourite of emperors and conquerors. Cyrus the Great, the Persian king, refounded the city and returned the Jewish exiles after conquering Babylon in 539 BCE. Alexander the Great had once made Jericho his personal estate way back in the fourth century BCE. Mark Antony had given Jericho as a gift to Cleopatra. Subsequently, Herod who got suzerainty over Jericho built a hippodrome in the town.

The town draws upon its religious heritage and archaeological relics to make up for its otherwise unremarkable contemporary character. We stroll through shops packed with Biblical mementos and touristy kitsch. A buffet spread of local bread piled with shredded carrots and beetroot constitutes our lunch although we top it up with a glass of the freshly squeezed juice of Jericho oranges—truly a drink fit for the gods.

Naif resumes his chatter as we whiz past bleak countryside to reach the Dead Sea. We don the regulation Dead Sea mud pack and slosh around a bit in the mucky, oily broth. Naif drives us to another historic site, the Tomb of Moses, before depositing us at the barbed-wire barricade with machine-gun-toting Israeli guards at Bethlehem from where we would make our way back to Jerusalem.

2013

Tokyo: Perched between Temples and Tech

Not only does the ATM promptly spit out my perfectly valid global cash card, but to add insult to injury, on the ATM screen, two comic figures—a boy and a girl—nod and bow their heads in commiseration. Try the machine a second time, and it beeps in panic. The comic figures have been replaced by squiggly Japanese characters blinking in red, which one presumes is a warning. Arriving at Narita, one of the most modern airports in the world, you would expect things to work better. Most ATMs refuse global cards. Currency-change counters are already closed and if you think you can swipe your credit card everywhere instead of handling unfamiliar currency—one that runs into tens of thousands even for simple purchases—think again. Except expensive outlets, the rest accept only cash in this city that prides itself as one of the finance capitals of the world. Outside Tokyo, it is virtually impossible to get by with only a credit card. Fortunately for me, my hotel has sent me pick-up.

My faith in Japanese technology is restored soon. The Japanese excel in the art of pampering your bottom, literally. While outside temperatures may plummet to below zero, loo seats are kept comfortably warm. An array of buttons, much like a console in a plane cockpit, serves up a variety of ablution options, at desired water temperatures. There are jets, squirts, trickle and drip options, if you go by the pictorial buttons. Sensors function like silent ghosts, switching on lights, activating the flush and faucets and so on. Initially, I was worried I'd scald my bottom if I pushed the wrong button, but was reassured by the concierge that the water temperature is always set to a comfortable 35 °C. In fact, wherever I went in Japan, my first challenge was to divine the faucet controls.

Tokyo dazzles, with its steel, glass and chrome high-rises, lit by neon lights and LEDs. Yet, this city does not intimidate the way Beijing does. Small-town Tokyo still peeks out of the forest of spires. Tiny houses with even tinier, in fact, postage stamp–sized, gardens line the narrow alleyways. Not a square inch of land is wasted in this densely populated country. Japanese diligence and attention to detail is evident everywhere right from the way the laundry is pegged to the lines to the artistic arrangement of tiny potted plants at the doorways of homes.

Tokyo's roads are narrow and hence run one on top of the other. It is still possible to walk or cycle on the lower levels, even on the high street. Scores of bikers, especially old women, confidently pedal away, doing their own shopping or chores. Never mind if it starts drizzling while you are pedalling. Just stop at one of the numerous vending machines that dispense umbrellas. Vending machines sell almost everything—from condoms to travel insurance, from eats and drinks to ice cream. If you find it difficult to figure out the denominations of coins below ¥100, you just scoop whatever coins you have and dump them into the machine which does the calculation for you and spits out the surplus.

It is easy to figure out the Tokyo Metro with its meticulous colour-coding and numbers. From Asakusa, home to the touristy Sensoji shrine, to the glitzy Ginza, Tokyo Metro almost makes taxis redundant. Everyone seems to be in a tearing hurry, yet, there is an underlying orderliness and courtesy. Or at least so we Indians might think. Tokyo Metro authorities, however, are not impressed. Metro stations sport eye-catching posters that exhort commuters to behave. From tongue-in-cheek teasers to pictorial representations of dos and don'ts, commuters are constantly reminded to behave.

I head to the ultimate pilgrimage destination for all Japanese. Yasukuni is a Shinto shrine established in 1869 for all those who laid down their lives in the Boshin War. Subsequently, in 1877, thousands of soldiers who put down the Satsuma rebels were also interred in the shrine under the orders of the then emperor of Japan. Yasukuni has evoked controversy for enshrining even war criminals along with other martyrs. The shrine authorities insist that they also served the emperor and hence deserve a place here. Protestors in black vans parked outside the shrine belt out music and distribute pamphlets to lodge their protest. The emperor, a shadowy but revered figure, lives next door behind the imposing walls of the imperial palace, and the protesters hope their message will reach him.

At all Japanese shrines and temples, there is a little tank with bamboo-handled water scoops for pilgrims to purify themselves before entering, much like we have in our temples. I am tempted to pilfer one of these objects of beauty, but it was too long to hide anywhere. The Japanese believe in reducing everything to writing— spoken words are transient. Inside the temple premises, there are designated prayer frames where devotees can hang their private message to the deity. The prayer frames are festooned with identical white chits (sold at the shrine itself), each with entreaties inscribed by the hands of the devotees. At the magnificent Meiji shrine, the beer-makers' guild has placed its offerings in the form of freshly brewed beer stacked in a row of casks.

Many of us have our own misconceptions about the Japanese, gleaned largely from manga comics. If you come to Tokyo expecting to see spiky-haired youngsters sporting psychedelic hair colour and pierced all over, you might be disappointed. Although fashion-conscious, Japanese boys and girls are generally soberly dressed. Manga comics have given way to mobile phones. And Japan seems to be the least adventurous, gastronomically too. Try finding international food—pizzas, pastas or burgers—outside of five-star hotels. Ramen rules. Restaurants have plastic mould reproductions of the food they sell, prominently displayed at the entrance. And the Japanese smilingly refuse to recognize or accommodate vegetarians. If you're the sort who dislikes seaweed or seafood or are a vegetarian, you might as well prepare to live on biscuits and fruit.

I make my way to greet Hachiko, the dog who waited for his master at Shibuya station every day for thirteen years. He did not know his master had been killed in an accident. Tokyoites have erected a statue for Hachiko in this busy square. It is a touching monument to a faithful friend, albeit of the quadruped variety. The busy Shibuya station millions of commuters cross every week, is now known as Hachiko square.

The high streets are full of young boys and girls who cajole pedestrians with their mellifluous sales pitches. In fact, calling out to customers is a rampant practice in Japan. Glitzy Ginza, once considered the rival of Champs-Élysées for hosting the maximum number of designer labels, has now bowed to other districts in this shopping-crazed city. I wrap up my visit to Tokyo with a quick trip to Sensō-ji temple (all temples have the suffix 'ji'). The temple is crowded with worshippers, all Japanese. Rice-cake stalls do brisk business. The route is lined with touristy kitsch. Incense wafts from giant vats. Large Japanese families spanning three or four generations are a common sight. After all, despite all its pretensions, Japan seems thoroughly Asian at heart.

2002

Hidden Treasures in Moreh

Gingerly stepping up a creaky ladder in the dark, we reach the penthouse, so to speak, of this three-storeyed thatch house. Maraikayar disappears into the dark depths below to re-emerge with a kerosene lantern that he hangs on a hook suspended from the bamboo rafter above. Then he vanishes again, leaving me alone in this gloomy room. The reluctant illumination casts eerie shadows on the thatch walls and reveals a freshly washed dhoti spread on a charpoy below. Cicadas are chirping lustily. Two lizards chase each other on the wall. There seems to be a mild drizzle outside. I am a bit uneasy wondering whether I should have accompanied him here at all.

But then, Maraikayar is back in a flash, this time with a small cloth bundle knotted at the top. With a flick of his wrist, he loosens the knot and shakes the contents of the parcel on to the white dhoti. Thousands of glittering gems—mostly pink Mogok rubies, but also some emeralds and blue sapphires—tumble out on to the dhoti and wink back at me in a blur of sparkles. I am mesmerized.

Surreal, and incongruous, considering the setting: a modest bamboo-and-thatch cottage built on stilts somewhere in the mosquito-ridden marshy backstreets of Moreh, a sleepy border town between Myanmar and Manipur. Maraikayar, a Tamil Muslim, has been a Moreh resident for over forty years now, and dabbles in everything from dosas to gems. Actually, I had come to his roadside eatery lured by the Tamil board outside which advertised dosas in this most unlikely corner of India, the Manipur–Myanmar border.

The dosa itself had been unremarkable, but our conversation was not. Maraikayar traced the history of the Tamil population in Moreh—they all came from the east, many on foot, trudging for months through the malarial jungles of what was then known as Burma, during the Second World War. Those days, there used to be a huge Tamil expat population in Malaysia, mostly traders. The lot comprised refugees fleeing Japanese-occupied lands, traders from Penang and beyond. When they reached the Indian border, some were too tired to trudge any farther and chose to settle down there. They went on to build their own Tamil schools, of which there are five now, and an equal number of Tamil temples. Garishly painted *Ayyanar*s, the *dwarapalaka*s of the Tamil pantheon, adorn the entrances to temples, and the *gopurams* could have been plucked out of interior towns in the deep south. The Tamil settlers in Moreh trade in ginger mostly, but also do a bit of smuggling on the side—mostly Chinese blankets, thermos flasks, torches and, perhaps, other contraband too. As I was leaving his eatery after my meal, Maraikayar asked me tentatively what my business in Moreh was and whether I would be interested in looking at some gems.

Back in his thatch hut now, he scoops a handful of similar-sized rubies and arranges them into a necklace on the dhoti. 'Take the lot—it's only 6500,' he says. He also tells me about a famous classical dancer who had come recently and picked up gemstones worth more than a lakh of rupees. He arranges another lot in the form of a bracelet. Unfortunately, I had not anticipated this cornucopia of sparklers in this most desolate corner of our land and had come unarmed with cash. Maraikayar, of course, would not trust me with credit even if it meant sending someone with me to Imphal where I could possibly arrange finance.

This was the year 2001. My trip to Manipur was to visit my husband who was posted there. After a few days in Imphal and Loktak, I still had a few more days to kill and hence decided to check out other places nearby. The Burmese border was just five hours away, and I was itching to see what a border town was like. Since hubby was too busy to go with me, I set out on my own, travelling from Imphal to Moreh on a rickety Sumo crammed with a dozen other passengers, alongside baskets of fowl and bundles of clothes and household items. It was a gruelling five-and-a-half-hour ride during which we were repeatedly stopped at numerous check posts and our vehicle inspected with exasperating precision by all manner of uniformed men, at times from paramilitary outfits, at others from the local police. Moreh is the very last town on the Indian side of the border.

Moreh, a frontier town in the boondocks, looked every bit its part. Swampy and mosquito-ridden, it was a picture of despair. But for the disenfranchised lot of Tamils who could not find a home in prosperous Malaya (in those days it used to be called Malaya and the Malayan Federation included Singapore as well), it was a land of opportunity.

Curiosity takes me to the other side of the border, a Myanmarese village called Tamu. You can cross the border check post—a waist-high cattle gate where a lone security official sells day passes costing Rs 10 each.

There are tuk-tuks waiting to ferry you to the village on the other side. Burmese girls draped in floral printed sarongs, with high cheekbones and cheeks smeared with bright *tanaka*, squeeze together into the tuk-tuk rattling its way to Tamu town through paddy fields and banana plantations. We soon alight in downtown Tamu. Vendors hawk sweet sticky rice cooked in bamboo poles. I make my way to the high street to see what it has to offer.

I can't believe my eyes. This tiny, nondescript village in a godforsaken corner of the jungle has a row of shops stocked to the gills with—you guessed it right—ruby-studded jewellery. There are bangles and necklaces, studs and tops, rings and bracelets, all glittering from inside their glass cases. There are also heaps of rubies and sapphires, cat's eye and peridot, jade and topaz, all neatly arranged in bowls and sold by the carat. I have never seen so much jewellery and so many gems in one place, not even in the jewellery section of Mustafa store in Singapore or G.R.T. Thanga Maligai in Chennai, both sprawling on football field–sized floors in their respective locations. I wonder who comes all the way to Tamu to pick up this exquisite and expensive jewellery. Obviously, they must be doing brisk business; why else would they be there? I count twenty-nine shops on the high street, but lose interest after that. Not when my wallet is so emaciated that all I can afford is a ride back to Imphal in that rickety Sumo.

2010

Shell-Shocked in Jordan

In the Hashemite Kingdom of Jordan, everything shuts down on Fridays—even buses. The few minibuses that do ply turn into millipedes by midday. They sprout several pairs of human legs, all sticking out from under the bus, toes pointing towards the sky, as though the critter has collapsed out of exhaustion. If you linger a few minutes, you realize why. The noon sun is hot enough to melt even metal; there's nary a shelter, not even a shrub or tree anywhere nearby for waiting passengers to hide. Minibuses, like those in Kolkata, must have a minimum number of passengers before they begin the trip. The most sensible thing to do for hopeful passengers is to dive under the belly of the bus until the number of passengers reaches a critical mass for the bus to get going.

On any other day, we (Kapil, my teenage son, and I) could have opted for a plush air-conditioned Volvo bus to reach my destination—Wadi Musa, the jumping-off point for Petra. But we happen to have landed in Amman on a Friday when everything comes to a standstill in the kingdom. We have no reservations in Amman, having planned to make it directly from Amman airport to Petra.

I blame our plight on H and A, our lovely hosts in Jerusalem, who helpfully dropped a series of hints: that Indian nationals get a Jordanian visa on arrival; that Amman is just an hour's flight from Jerusalem; that since we were flying Royal Jordanian in any case, organizing a stopover in Jordan for a few days on our return trip should be a breeze; that Petra is a drop-dead gorgeous destination, a must-do on any self-respecting traveller's bucket list. To be fair to them, they did this only after a week when, like the proverbial Indian *atithi*, we had displayed few signs of budging from their hospitable home smack in the heart of Jerusalem. I bit the bait, promptly. Our gracious hosts even dropped us off at the Jerusalem airport, just to make sure. Perhaps H knew Friday is a holiday in Jordan, but I want to give him the benefit of the doubt.

If I had been the right gender and a little more agile, I would have been tempted to add my own pair of legs to the line-up under the minibus, but for the present, I had no option but to wilt in the baking desert sun, cussing and swearing, ruing my foolishness in venturing into a foreign country impromptu, without doing any homework. It takes two hours for the beat-up jalopy to fill up.

Eventually, we get going. We, being the lone foreigners on the bus today, are given the seat of honour, next to the sizzling and shuddering bonnet haphazardly covered with a Rexine cushion. The roads in Jordan are no doubt excellent, but every time the bus hits a speed breaker—of which there seem to be an inordinate number, quite unnecessarily, if you ask me—my thigh or shin gets toasted through my thin trousers, leaving angry welts on my skin. Like our own minibuses, this one too had stuck windows which wouldn't shut, turning the inside of the bus into an air fryer. When I try to shift away from the bonnet, I put one foot inadvertently into a basket of soporific fowl that panic, cluck furiously and start spilling out and flying about, much to the merriment of the other passengers and the consternation of the owner. The live missiles are caught and returned to the basket and covered with a red cloth.

Petra rocks!

After four hours of this torture, the bus deposits us in Wadi Musa on the edge of the desert where we go looking for a hotel. For a town in the boondocks, its high street is littered with star chains—in fact, the highest concentration of five-star hotels anywhere in the world. We eye the Mövenpicks and Marriotts warily and look for a modest hotel that would not stress my slender wallet. We choose one that seems to be hiding in a side street, check in, dump our luggage and go in search of vegetarian fare.

By now the weather has cooled down quite a bit. After some wandering, we locate a local bakery—a mechanized one that spits out one *non* a minute. We gape as non after non falls with a gentle thud on to the floor. Each is instantly picked up and handed over to the waiting customers. We grab a couple and buy a jar of hummus in the grocery. Our dinner is done, I announce cheerily, even as Kapil looks longingly at the shawarma rolls spinning like Buddhist prayer wheels. So I let him gorge on the Jordanian goat meat while I chew on my stringy non.

Wandering through the ruins of Petra is exciting, and not merely on account of the stunning Al-Khazneh and the graphic art on rocks.

Carved out of a single rock and an imposing 40 metres high, Al-Khazneh (or Khasneh al-Faroun) is named after a Bedouin legend that spoke of a treasure hidden by a pharaoh in an urn on top. Even today, the urn sports many bullet holes from those who tried to bring it down to retrieve the treasure. In reality, however, Al-Khazneh is a funerary monument, possibly the mausoleum of King Aretas (IV) who reigned from 9 BCE to 40 CE. Funerary symbols related to afterlife and death adorn the monument.

Your ticket to the complex includes a camel carriage ride all the way to the ruins, a good kilometre-long trudge in the desert sun, but as you enter through the ostentatious gates there's nary a carriage in sight. It is only after you have covered the entire distance on foot that you spot local transport.

In their heyday, Nabateans may have been adept at harnessing precious water, but today all you can get, as you simmer and singe your way to the ruins, is bottled Evian. I shell out a king's ransom for a bottle. The shopkeeper gets a call on his mobile which he presses to his flowing headgear and hurriedly strides out. I watch, jaw wide open, as he gets into his Mercedes parked outside the complex and drives off somewhere, leaving his shop to the care of his assistant.

Petra, now surviving only through its sprawling ruins, used to be a flourishing trading city of the Nabateans, a desert civilization. Before them were the Edomites (from *edom* meaning red rock) who lived in the region around 1200 BCE. They carried on a flourishing trade in spices and frankincense, could weave exquisite textiles, craft pottery and were skilled in metalwork. The Nabateans followed the Edomites almost 600 years later and made Petra their capital, drawing upon their ability to harness water through their superior hydraulic-engineering skills. Nabatean ingenuity enabled them to transform this barren rocky terrain into a bustling bazaar doing brisk business, and the land around it fecund enough to sustain the city's resident and itinerant population. The Nabateans managed to coax flood and spring water through channels and underground tunnels, store it in cisterns and reservoirs and direct it to palaces and settlements.

Striations in a tomb in Petra

History may have consigned Petra's past to amnesia, but traders do their best to keep it alive. Once you have reached the ruins, dodging dogged donkey taxis that offer to take you through the obstacle race of the sprawling complex for an extortionate fare calls for all the skills you honed to perfection in the by-lanes of Chawri Bazar. It takes an Indian to haggle down a persistent hawker trying to pass off plastic as *firouzeh*—precious turquoise, found ubiquitously in the desert and used extensively in jewellery. Every hidden nook and cranny in this rocky paradise is colonized by hawkers who ambush you with their ersatz Nabatean artefacts: a deliberately dented and carefully patina-ed teapot, fashioned in the back lanes of Wadi Musa last week, is thrust in your face as you turn a blind corner; a tin necklace studded with pebbles is touted as one belonging to the Nabatean queen. But we manage to escape unscathed.

Wait, did I congratulate myself too soon? After a couple of days in Petra, we are back at Amman airport to board the flight home. Immigration and security done, we are ambling to our boarding gate when I hear my son's name mangled beyond recognition on the PA system. We hurry back to the assigned counter, where, without a word, Kapil, all of seventeen is whisked away beyond immigration back into Jordan while I am left standing on this side of the gate, in utter panic. Minutes tick away and there's still no sign of him. I wring my hands in anxiety, but the woman behind the counter is inscrutable. The security guards look too fierce for me to make a dash back into Jordan.

After about fifteen minutes of this agonizing wait, Kapil and a smartly uniformed officer appear at a distance. A helper is wheeling Kapil's suitcase, its zip ripped apart and its contents threatening to spill on to the marbled floor of the airport. Kapil's face is ashen. The officer explains to me that they found a shell in his suitcase and want me to explain why. It showed up in the X-ray and in a jiffy they had smoothly run the tip of a ball pen through the zip of his suitcase to prise it open and retrieve the offending object. It is an empty shell that he had picked up at a parking lot in Jerusalem, a tiny, shiny, metal object of the kind that fascinates a typical teenager. Without a thought, he had shoved it into his shorts pocket. It has come to haunt us now.

All over Israel, youngsters conscripted compulsorily carry their guns everywhere, even to restaurants and shops. Many of them wear belts of ammunition too, a novelty for a young kid unused to seeing so much firepower all at once.

After much explanation and cajoling, the officer relents and agrees to let us go provided Kapil signs some documents. All this on the other side of the immigration gate. A distraught Kapil is whisked back to a desk on the far side and made to sign several papers before being let off with much index-finger-wagging. Till date, he has no clue what he had signed on that fateful day.

2009

Pushkar: Creation in All Forms

Pushkar, congested, crowded and dirty by day, is magically transformed by evening. Come dusk, the quotidian makes way for the exotic, exciting and mystical in this temple town sacred to Hindus and junkies of all denominations. The ghats, swarming with bathers and seekers of spiritual salvation, become bereft and silent as night falls. Another breed, seekers of a different kind of salvation, emerge out of the shadows; the gullies and lanes are now enveloped in a haze from their chillums. Elsewhere, harmoniums and tablas vie with guitars to produce a cacophony that rends the stillness of the night.

Pushkar, the temple town in Rajasthan, 400-odd km from Delhi, is many things to many people. For the devout, it is the ultimate pilgrimage destination with its holy Brahma temple, the only one in the world dedicated

to the Hindu god of creation. The fabled waters of the
lake are believed to wash away the sins of the faithful
who journey patiently from far and near just to take a
dip in its murky waters. For the tattooed and bedraggled
youth from Europe and Israel who come hurtling down
the town's narrow winding roads on their bikes and
motorcycles, Pushkar holds out the irresistible allure
of nirvana of a different kind—one that enters the
soul through the miasma of psychotropic smoke or the
intravenous needle!

Serene Puskhar lake framed by the Aravallis

Pushkar draws also the savvy trader and the bargain
hunter, especially during the famous Pushkar Mela where
tens of thousands of cattle and camels gather in the largest

livestock exchange in this part of the world. While farmers and ranchers do their deals in the mela, the bargain hunters from boutiques in Delhi and Jaipur descend on this town to pick up silver jewellery, leather crafts, puppets and antique household objects; these will be carefully patina-ed so that they fetch antique prices in the fashionable districts of Mumbai or Bengaluru. And finally, there are people like me who wander into this town out of curiosity to glimpse a fading way of life in the desert town—one in which pleasure still means leisure, and lazing around is not equated with debauchery!

Shopfronts sport brightly coloured puppets, their limbs dangling languorously. Cowbells clang as camel-drawn carts puff up the sandy slopes. Motorcycles slung about with milk cans and mounted by handsome men in oversize turbans hoot stridently, scattering helter-skelter pedestrians and street dogs alike. From a perfumery laden with vials of multitudinous sizes wafts the heady fragrance of a million roses; but even this cannot camouflage the odour of cow dung and urine that pervades Pushkar. Roadside eateries, right beside garbage heaps, do brisk business in *malpua*s floating in sickly-looking syrup. Distant drumbeats advertise evening *aarti* in one of the numerous temples that abound in this town. There are of course mendicants galore—bearded, half-naked, barefoot, ash-smeared, beady-eyed, all in search of prasad—of some kind. Wherever you turn, Pushkar assaults your senses as only an Indian temple town can.

Of course, having driven all the way from Delhi, we hurry for the regulation darshan of Brahma temple. When I stop to buy prasad to offer to Brahma, the shopkeeper, who had been blithely munching the prasad from his own basket, hastily wipes his mouth and measures out the sugar-coated puffed rice crispies for me. I wonder how much he manages to sell if he stuffs himself like this every day. While he is busy with this transaction, a street dog grabs a mouthful of jalebis, also meant to be prasad.

Next day we go in pursuit of some good karma—bathe in the lake and perform puja. The priest who officiates at the puja used to be a postman until recently. He tells us how the lake turned up millions of dead fish the previous year and the whole town stank for weeks! I spy flotsam— rotten garlands and detritus. We pretend not to notice and take a dip. A cow burrows its snout into the pile of my clothes lying on the steps of the ghat. Watching the cow from the water, my prayers to the presiding deity at Pushkar turn from the sublime to the mundane. 'Oh God, please don't let the cow eat my sari!'

Having got the puja and holy dip out of the way, we are free to explore the many delights that Pushkar has to offer. We make our way to the edge of the desert just in time to glimpse the splatter of orange that the setting sun has carelessly dripped on the desert sky. The orange turns golden as the sun dips behind a sand knoll and the streak spreads across the horizon. But it is fronted by a festoon of plastic bags and a dead crow dangling from the electric wires. How did the polythene bags get so high up, I wonder. A political procession wends its way along the streets, kicking up dust and raising slogans. Geriatric American tourists haggle raucously with shopkeepers to buy fake ruby and silver jewellery.

The next day, we wrap up our visit to Pushkar with a wobbly ride on a rogue camel that keeps drooling streams of saliva and dangerously lurching to dislodge me. I hold on to its hump for dear life and concentrate fully on not being thrown off. When I manage to complete the ride with my limbs intact, I feel as if I too have attained nirvana at last, Pushkar style!

2006

Punctured Andalusian Dreams

You might plan a trip to Andalusia, seduced by any or all of the following: Alhambra, Granada's Moorish jewel; Mesquita, Cordoba's gorgeous mosque with its striped arches and doorways; Giralda, Seville's towering minaret, crowned, rather incongruously, with a Christian belfry; endless olive groves; energetic Flamenco dances; eloquent operas like Rossini's *Barber of Seville*; esoteric novels like Paul Coelho's *The Alchemist*.

But don't let your imagination run riot. When my friend R and I land in Seville late one evening, what we find is a dreary town with uninspiring concrete blocks. The romantic-sounding Guadalquivir is nothing but a foul ditch winding its way through the town's congested streets. Our little boutique hotel downtown is neither boutique nor a hotel. It is a glorified homestay, grossly overpriced, over-ornate and under-occupied. No, make it unoccupied. We are the only guests here. This was before the time of Airbnb.

The manager-cum-owner of the property is a surly, pot-bellied man who gleefully informs us that the establishment has no boarding facilities and if we need a bite to eat we have to trudge all the way to the high street several blocks away. Booking rooms on the Internet is not unlike going on a blind date. You take what comes. He looks us up and down and, with a leer, asks us if we need a double bed or two singles.

The bungalow is pretentious, with brocade curtains and silken drawstrings. When you open the curtains, all you see is a concrete wall. The place smells un-lived-in, musty, which the recently applied room freshener scarcely conceals. When R shuts the door of our room, she finds a tag hanging from the doorknob. Turning it around, she reads aloud, '*Ne molestar*'. 'Wonder why they have to declare this? Perhaps it is customary to molest women guests in this country? Do you think the steep tariff for this dump of a hotel is because of this assurance of safety?' she asks earnestly. I am tickled. Although my knowledge of the Spanish language is nil, from the position of the tag, I presume it is a 'Do Not Disturb' sign to be hung on the doorknob if you want to sleep late. In this forlorn lodge that does not even offer breakfast, it seems pretentious and unnecessary.

It's almost midnight when we make our way to the much-touted Andalusian 'tapas bar', drooling in anticipation of the epicurean delights that await us. It turns out to be a noisy, overcrowded, smoke-filled bistro serving an array of indifferent snacks! Worse, we are charged double for everything we order, and a volley of Spanish arguments—abuses I presume—pours forth when we point this out. Boy, the Spaniards can speak really fast, accompanied by expansive gestures, and never let you get a word in edgewise.

But indifferent snacks and apathetic service don't seem to deter the locals. And they are dressed to kill. Trendy women with backless and strapless dresses float in and out of tapas bars balancing on 6-inch stilettos. R and I seem to be the only women here with our shoulders covered and heels flat, so to speak. We feel suitably matronly and hopelessly out of place and beat a hasty retreat to the square where we can merge into the shadows and make ourselves less visible.

But the square is so brightly illuminated that we stick out like a sore thumb in our frumpy attire. As if to accentuate our frumpiness, a newly-wed couple floats past, she in a dazzling white sequinned gown and he in a black tuxedo, clutching her rose bouquet for her. We wonder what this couple is doing here in the square at this hour instead of cosying up in their bridal suite and doing what honeymooners do best.

The next day, we huff and puff our way to the top of the Giralda, the minaret, through a ramp on which horsemen rode in earlier times, my lens poised to capture the stunning view of Seville town it is purported to offer. Built in the late twelfth century, the Giralda, a lofty, aesthetically carved tower, is Spain's most perfect Islamic monument. The belfry, a later-day Christian imposition, holds El Giraldillo, a weathervane that is also the symbol of Seville. Just as we reach the top, the bells of the cathedral start pealing, almost knocking us off balance. The camera flies off my hands and violently pulls on my neck, almost snapping it. Amidst the deafening clamour of the bell, we clumsily clamber back on to our feet and run back and down as fast as our arthritic limbs allow us. So much for our Seville trip.

2007

'Tranziting' through the Czech Republic

As I check into the elegant Schlosshotel Cecilienhof, in Potsdam near Berlin, I rue the timing of my visit, which happens to be on a cold, grey day in October. The skies are ominously gloomy, portending a storm. But then, I have little control over the timing or location (this applies to most of my visits), both of which are decided by the conference organizers, determined, no doubt, by the bargain-basement tariffs offered by hotels during off-season. Fretfully I saunter around the premises, and stray into the adjoining wing of the hotel, now a fascinating museum. Indeed, this was the historic location where three great statesmen—Harry Truman, Winston Churchill and Josef Stalin—met in 1945 to carve out the future contours of post-war Europe. Little would they have imagined that their division of spoils would unravel messily within decades. The hotel had leveraged the event to great advantage, showcasing the interesting memorabilia from the meeting and a wealth of priceless sepia images.

Schlosshotel Cecilienhof where Churchill, Truman and Stalin met in 1945 to decide the future of Germany

But there is only so much you can see in a museum. With what I believed to be wise aforethought, I had booked my return ticket to Delhi a few days after the conference just so that I could hang out in trendy reincarnated East Berlin and join the tourists gaping at the Brandenburg Gate or Checkpoint Charlie—perhaps even bring back home a piece of the infamous Wall itself which survives mostly as bits of concrete in souvenir shops.

Now that the storm is upon us, Berlin is out. I need to find ways to spend the next three days fruitfully. After all, a Schengen visa is not easy to obtain. I scan the map in the hotel lobby for sunnier destinations accessible to my emaciated wallet. Prague seems near enough. The receptionist informs me it is just five hours away by train, that there are several trains a day to Prague and that I should have no difficulty in getting there. She also checks the weather in Prague and assures me it is unaffected by the storm. Back in my room, I Google and check the website of the Embassy of the Czech Republic in Delhi and find out that Indian citizens holding a multi-entry Schengen visa can 'transit' through the Czech Republic.

Voila, that's what I decide to do. I dump my luggage in a locker at Berlin Hauptbahnhof and board a train for the Czech Republic. It is virtually empty and I have a whole coach to myself. Who would want to travel in this kind of weather? We cruise along the Elbe River. A picture-postcard Bohemian landscape unfolds. The sun struggles to break free of the clouds, intermittently bathing the countryside in its golden rays. What more can I ask for?

A lot more, as I soon find out, when a portly Czech immigration official boards the train at Decin on the German–Czech border. He asks me where I propose to go from Prague. Eager to assure him of my honourable intention to not jump visa and disappear into a subterranean universe of undocumented, unwanted aliens—the scourge and support staff of Europe—I tell him I have to fly back to New Delhi from Berlin and hence would be returning to Berlin in a couple of days, probably by the same train.

His impassive countenance gives way to an ominous frown. He pores over the visa page of my passport for a few more seconds, and pronounces, with a sickening tone of finality, that my visa did not allow me that luxury. I can only 'tranzit' through the Czech Republic, which means I need to exit through another Schengen country. He might have detrained me, but the train had already moved quite a distance into the Czech countryside by now. Getting rid of me would involve elaborate logistics of finding transport to take me back into Germany. Reluctantly he stamps my passport with that dreaded word 'tranzit' and hands over my passport, wagging his finger and warning me not to come back this way. At the next station, he jumps off on the platform and leaves me to wallow in my anxiety.

This being 2007, Schengen was still an evolving agreement. I haven't the foggiest idea as to which countries are part of the European Union, leave alone the subset Schengen. Does Slovakia qualify to be a member of this august agreement? Which countries count as Eastern Europe? Geography had never been my strength, what with all those indecipherable maps and rainfall patterns. I had a vague idea that some countries were already in, while others were waiting to be admitted—whoever paid any attention to these irrelevant bits of information on the international pages of newspapers anyway? Would the adjoining Schengen country be Austria? Or was it Poland?

I can no longer enjoy the gorgeous landscape framed within my train window. My mind is a cauldron of cartographic confusion. Racing through my imagination are different permutations and combinations of European countries, their borders outrageously distorted, no doubt, but with the Czech Republic at the centre of the scheme. I will have to consult Dr Google to put me out of my misery. Unfortunately, I have neither a foreign SIM nor data on my cell phone to do that right away. That will be the first thing I'll do when I get to my hotel—if I get to my hotel—in Prague.

Four hours later, the train chugs into Prague Central. I am approached by a tout, an old woman who offers to take me to a budget hotel in the old town for a modest fee. Normally I would have brushed off such offers and wasted much time locating one myself, but today I am in a hurry to get to a hotel. I accompany her and she deposits me in a sleazy budget hotel close to the city centre, grandiosely named Manhattan Hotel.

Dr Google has bad news for me. The only other Schengen state that shares a border with the Czech Republic is Austria. Salzburg, the Austrian border town, is at least seven hours away by train and it's another twelve hours from there to Berlin! I quickly check the flight options and find them way too expensive. I have two options now: either to skip Prague, keep travelling through Czech territory by bus or train and reach Austria and continue on to Berlin which I might reach just in time for my flight back home. Or just risk the wrath of Czech immigration officials, and stay on in lovely Prague and face the consequences! I opt for the latter.

Being in the Bohemian capital on a sunny winter day is unparalleled joy. There are few tourists about although, according to locals, this winter has been the mildest in the collective Czech memory. The temperature is a balmy 14 °C. The Vltava, a tributary of the Elbe, snakes through central Prague splattered with Gothic, Baroque, Rococo and Jewish architecture. Many elegant bridges span the river, but none so ornamental or ancient as the Charles Bridge, the spirit and soul of Bohemia. It is exquisitely studded with statuary, evoking the aesthetics of the Baroque era. There is a live band playing the best of Czech composers. The night is crisp and the bridge is lively with locals and visitors admiring the glittering lights reflected in the tranquil waters of the Vltava. Sadly, I am unable to appreciate this feast for the eyes and the ears. Like a cracked gramophone record, there is just one tune playing repeatedly in my mind—what if I am detained on my way out and miss my return flight?

It is a Saturday when I locate the number and call up the Indian embassy in Prague in sheer desperation. After a lot of conniving and cajoling, I manage to get through to the Ambassador himself at his residence. Appropriately contrite, I narrate my predicament, but he is unmoved. Had I informed him prior to entering the country, he might have been able to do something, but now there is little the embassy could do for me.

Distraught, I saunter aimlessly through Europe's largest square, Wenceslas Square. Or at least so the tourist pamphlets claim. Originally a horse market, this square was named for Saint Wenceslas, a Bohemian prince. The square seems to have witnessed a lot of political action through its long history, such as the national movement of the nineteenth century, of the Declaration of Czech Independence of 1918, of Nazi muscle-flexing, political demonstrations, immolation, vandalism, the works. Today it looks innocuously sleazy and unabashedly commercial. I enter a cafe and order hot wine, that typical Czech specialty to cure you of un-Bohemian anxiety!

On Monday, I am back at Prague Central. Now comes the tricky part. What if the ticket attendant asks to see my passport? How do I buy a ticket without getting caught? I lounge around the railway station waiting for a suitable accomplice to accomplish this mission. The same tout who led me to my hotel on my arrival is shuffling towards the entrance. I accost her and press down a €5 bill into her palm and request her to get me a ticket. She is only too happy to oblige; after all, this is easier than escorting cantankerous foreigners to the city centre and trudging from one sleazy inn to another, just to earn the same amount.

I am back on the train to Berlin, which, again, is virtually empty and I am too conspicuous, for merely being in it. I curse the Europeans who can afford to run empty trains so many times a day to destinations where few people want to go. I consider hiding under the seat, but it is too narrow for my bulk. Next I target the washroom. The light above the toilet lights up red the moment you shut the door. That means I can't hide in there either. There is no option but to be a sitting duck, literally.

At Decin, the dreaded Czech immigration official, a woman this time, boards the train. She seems to have at least one customer to inspect. After scrutinizing my passport thoroughly, she turns aggressive. 'Didn't my *colega* tell you you can't go back to Berlin?' She towers over me and glowers. I cower and fish out my return ticket and wave it on her face. If I miss my flight, I will be the guest of the Czech government, for God knows how long. I lapse into a rapturous description of how beautiful Prague was and how much I enjoyed seeing their lovely city. She is unmoved. I resign myself to the prospect of being detrained and detained on foreign soil. After a few excruciating minutes of stony silence when we face each other as in a pantomime, she suddenly asks me, 'So you're transiting through Czech Republic a second time?' I nod appreciatively. After all, she needs a valid reason to let me off. She stamps my passport with a second 'tranzit' and tosses it on my lap. I heave a sigh of relief! The Bohemian countryside is beautiful again.

Teetering between Myth and Reality in Yingkiong

A cheerful Siang is gurgling away, some 300 feet below my own two feet that straddle the ominously sagging bridge. No, I am not standing on one of those metal suspension bridges, but astride an artisanal prototype made up entirely of single-origin bamboo and ropes. It is an ingenious contraption, an engineering marvel of sorts, conceived and executed entirely by local villagers, using indigenous materials: home-grown jute, rattan and bamboo. But it serves their purpose—of avoiding a five-hour trudge to reach markets on this side of the river.

The ropes on the bridge are so loosely bound that the gaps between the knots are large enough to send your considerable bulk crashing through, into the swirling waters below. The floor of the bridge, also made up of jute ropes, is helpfully covered with pieces of jagged wooden planks. Since the planks are not, and cannot be, nailed anywhere, every time you step on one edge, the other edge lifts up like a see-saw, leaving you hanging on to the ropes in sheer terror. Your own steely nerves hardly make up for the absence of steel in the bridge.

Swaying bridge over a swirling Siang

We had no idea of all this when Pema, the smart and helpful official from Yingkiong administration, suggested we send our vehicle ahead through the rutted road leading to Tuting. It would take five hours for the vehicle to reach the other bank of the river. Once it arrived, we could cross from the Yingkiong side to the other bank through this infamous rope bridge and be on our way. Incidentally, it would give us five more hours in quaint Yingkiong, which we could use to visit the local attractions. Who can refuse such well-intentioned and persuasive advice? We comply.

R and I are headed for Tuting and Gelling, frontier villages in Arunachal Pradesh on this side of the border with China, to glimpse the Great Bend of the Yarlung Tsangpo before it enters India, where it is rechristened Siang. Visions of the cascades through which the river leaps down the Great Bend have haunted me for several months now, after I had listened to river experts waxing eloquent on this unique phenomenon in various seminars in Delhi. Which is why, when we get an opportunity to visit Duliajan in Assam, I jump at the opportunity to check it out. R joins me on this adventure. Our indulgent hosts in Duliajan are helpful enough to arrange a sturdy four-wheel drive for the trip up to the border. What they don't tell us and probably don't even know, since they themselves seldom stir out of their comfort zone, is that there is no proper road to the border except a rutted, dusty path washed away in parts by the monsoon. There are no buses plying on this route—only an occasional SUV taxi hired by crazy outsiders. Even the locals take the weekly chopper flight rather than endure the ride.

Pema tells us Yingkiong markets will open only after a couple of hours and advises us to wait in the circuit house until she can arrange someone to accompany us. We return reluctantly to our room to relive the nightmarish memories of previous evening, when our vehicle wheezed and sputtered on a precipitous ledge on the mountainside.

It was an eerie night when any moment we expected to plunge headlong into the bottomless ravine on the other side. Hadn't we read that like the Great Bend itself, the gorges in these parts are twice as deep as the Grand Canyon? It is a miracle we reached safely.

After roaming the streets of the spectacularly located Yingkiong town—it is surrounded by mountains on all sides—and visiting the produce market dominated by women, we return to the bridge around 3 p.m. Our vehicle is already there. Our driver waves to us from the other bank. Having sent across our luggage in the vehicle, we can now cross unencumbered by our bags, but I still have my camera and lens dangling around my neck.

I send R ahead. Being an intrepid *sardarni*, she is unfazed by the sagging, swinging contraption. Holding on

R, holding on to dear life on the shaky rope bridge

to the loose ropes on the sides, she bravely steps on the bridge and walks purposefully across, undeterred by the see-saw plank. I follow gingerly, trying not to look down between the ropes, but the blessed river is wherever you look. The bridge sways, at first gently, but soon, violently.

About a third of the way, I lift my head to see a steady stream of villagers coming over from the other end towards us. One woman carries a big bundle on her head, another, a baby strapped to her back and several other villagers with bags, all headed for the 3.30 bus that would leave from Yingkiong to another similar godforsaken destination, no doubt. For them, crossing the bridge is daily life, their only link to so-called civilization.

Every time we stop to let a villager pass, the bridge sags and sways some more, threatening to dislodge everyone, but they smile indulgently and move on. I manage to stop midway to click R's picture for posterity. Step by painful step, we manage to cross over to the other side where a very steep climb up a hillside dotted with bramble awaits us. We clamber on all fours, lacerated and breathless. As soon as I am safely up on the other bank, I turn back to admire my feat, only to let out a scream. A man on a motorcycle, both legs stretched out away from the pedals for balance, is gliding through the swinging bridge, frowning in intense concentration. My shrieking disturbs him. But he manages to keep his control and is already on this bank, expertly guiding his bike up the steep slope. My jaw remains open for the rest of the day.

Soon we are on our way in our SUV, virtually making our own road through the wilderness. Although it is not yet 4 p.m., the sun goes down rapidly and it is already twilight. On one side of the road is a deep gorge, one through which an unseen Siang flows, and on the other, the hillside dotted with tropical vegetation, mostly banana trees and palms. There is no settlement between here and Tuting, which is a good four hours away, and we are driving into primordial wilderness. The rutted path is a river of slush, thanks to the torrential rains of the past week. There are places where the path cleaves in two, leaving us wondering which fork to take. Soon, it is inky dark, the only source of light being our own headlights and the dashboard, which cast eerie reflections on the vegetation, hoodwinking you into believing there are well-lit houses out there. We are literally driving off the map. For the first time in days, I sense apprehension gripping me. Am I being foolhardy, undertaking a venture like this for some illusory Great Bend that no one seems to have set eyes on?

After six hours of bumping through the inky blackness, we arrive at Tuting, a village wrapped in more inky blackness. The total population is 600, all of whom have made their peace with the fact that electric connectivity and supply are two different things. We check into its derelict circuit house piled high with broken furniture everywhere and fall into a fitful slumber. In the morning, we go around this frontier town to reconfirm our impressions of the previous night. There is virtually no activity here, not even cultivation. With nature dishing out bananas and edible roots and vegetables, the villagers seem happy enough to just live off the land.

From our Tuting abode, nothing is visible. We now have to trudge at least a couple of hours to reach the high point called Gelling from where the river will reveal itself. When we reach the high point, all I can see is a tame Siang, no wider than 10 feet, wending its way sinuously into Indian territory. The Great Bend is nowhere to be seen; in fact, no bend is seen anywhere. It must be beyond that chain of mountains yonder. If at all it exists, it must be in Chinese territory. We have no permission to go even an inch farther. The many cascades through which the river leapt down into Indian territory (according to water experts) are nowhere to be seen. Did I not hear water pundits wax eloquent on how the cascades capture all the precipitation on the Indian side, adding to the flow of the water?

Disappointed, we make our way back to Tuting. Fortunately, the weekly helicopter comes today and R and I are happy to find ourselves on it, amidst bundles and bags of assorted sizes. There is much sneezing and coughing and visibly sick local residents travelling all the way to Dibrugarh to get some medical help. What are we complaining about?

The two pilots, one in his fifties and the other younger, are happy to chat with us while the chopper is being loaded. They both hail from Delhi too. The flight is a memorable one, cruising low over some pristine jungles and mountains in a remote region of our vast country. Months later, we read in the newspapers that the flight from Yingkiong crashed due to bad weather, killing everybody on board, including the two pilots whom we had befriended. Saddened and chastened, we look back on a trip we had probably dreamt up . . .

On the Roof of the World

Already bitten once, I should have been shy the second time. But I am a sucker for long road trips—I like nothing better than rolling wheels under my bottom. So, in 2013, when I was invited to join an all-expenses-paid 5000-km, three-week road trip through the 'stans', I could not resist it, despite the Nikitin fiasco. Besides, this one was being organized by my friends at the India Central Asia Foundation (ICAF), an organization with deep roots and abundant goodwill in those areas, and as such bode a smooth trip. This journey held out the promise of lofty views from atop the Pamirs and Altais, Hindu Kush and Tien Shan and tantalized with the chance to glimpse the pastoral idyll of nomadic peoples who inhabit these remote mountains. It would take us through heritage towns like Andijon, Bukhara, Samarkand and Khiva, and other such relatively unexplored regions of the planet.

The flip side, of course, was that this trip would be peppered with frequent stops in research institutes and think tanks along the way, not to mention mind-numbing seminars, soul-stilling speeches and never-ending toasts in official banquets. Well, there are no free lunches as they say! How the organizers managed to gather a disparate and mismatched group of fifteen idiosyncratic individuals on a trip like this is a mystery, but it spiced up the trip, at the least. Here we were, three frumpy middle-aged women (including this writer), roped in for their perceived expertise in matters Central Asian; three ultra-fashionable young ladies just out of their twenties, changing attires and accessories faster than models on ramps, included in the group for their imagined skills in film-making (more on this, later); and an equal number of arthritic senior citizens hobbling along, reeking of pain balms. Three other younger men who held the team together and oversaw all arrangements made up the complement. Unlike the Nikitin expedition, the ICAF trip would hire local vehicles in each country which would save the organizers the bother of obtaining the expensive Carnet de Passage.

On a fine morning, all of us landed in Astana. In many ways Astana was a stark contrast to places that followed in our itinerary. The city shivered in subzero temperatures in the month of September while the rest of Central Asia basked in celebratory summer weather. Astana is the spanking new capital of Kazakhstan, built with all the lavishness that only oil wealth can afford; it had none of the charm of old cities like Almaty or Bishkek or the grace of historical towns like Bukhara or Khiva. The town rose like a giant plastic Legoland in the middle of a bereft steppe otherwise incapable of supporting human habitation. Entirely artificial constructs, Astana's gleaming skyscrapers, festooned with glittering fairy lights, seemed all the more unreal because of the absence of people on its streets. Its broad and neatly laid-out avenues, glitzy plazas and snazzy shopping malls looked more like a gargantuan film set minus the actors than a living city. Oil wealth can certainly build new capitals—Nigeria built Abuja and Myanmar Naypyitaw—but it takes people to put life and soul into cities. Astana, established only in 1997, had not yet caught up in 2013.[1]

We stopped in Temirtau, the steel city. Lakshmi Mittal's Arcelor produced three million tons of steel, most of which went towards building the skyscrapers in Astana, 220 km away. After the dazzling perfection of Astana, Temirtau was comfortingly Indian. The hotel we stayed in was owned by Mittal and served Indian food alongside Kazakh and Russian fare. Mittal also ran a power plant that burnt coal from its own mines not far away. His company supplied water, electricity and steam to the city, and ran the town's tram services. Mittal also owned hospitals and schools. ArcelorMittal and its subsidiaries provided

---

1   At the time of writing in 2018, Astana had become the second largest city in Kazakhstan, with over a million residents.

employment to around 35,000 people in Temirtau, of which persons of Indian origin were just a handful—at the top. Incidentally, Nursultan Nazarbayev, the late President of Kazakhstan, began his career as a worker in a steel plant in Temirtau.

The drive through the empty stretches of Kazakhstan brought us to the Chinese border in Xinjiang. While the expedition had no visas to enter China, the ICAF magic worked to whisk us across the border into a town called Khorgos. The town was a fantasy in the middle of nowhere. It was a beehive of activity with construction cranes crowding the horizon. A steady stream of Kazakhs queued up at the immigration booth, waiting to cross into China and return with manufactured goods to market back home in Almaty and other towns. The Chinese were eager to show off what they had done to Khorgos, now crowded with commercial complexes, casinos, hotels, hospitals, malls, theatres, sports stadia, etc., sprawled over more than 500 hectares straddling both the countries. But where were the people who would use all these world-class facilities, we wondered. Having visited other Chinese border towns like Ruilly on the Myanmar border, I realized most of it was for demonstration, not actual use. A neat ribbon of road, smooth as silk, led up to Turfan and beyond in Xinjiang. We had met quite a few shoppers from Almaty picking up everything from mobile phones to tyres and silk scarves in the sole mall that had just been opened. The three young ladies in our group lapped up fancy clothing, handbags and footwear as if they were not already carrying mountains of stuff on this journey.

Sandwiched between the endless steppes of Kazakhstan and the barren desert landscape that makes up most of Uzbekistan, Kyrgyz Republic was a haven of verdure. Almost 80 per cent of the country is mountainous but the hills are interspersed with expansive pastures and lush valleys. Arable land is limited to the fertile Fergana Valley in the south, shared with neighbouring Uzbekistan.

Exquisitely proportioned carriages on display in the Museum of Regional Studies in Kokand, Fergana

It was therefore natural that Kirghizia had traditionally been home to nomadic tribesmen and women who kept moving with their portable yurts (cloth tent dwellings of nomads) and livestock. The horse and the soaring condor were their sole means of transportation and communication respectively until almost the twentieth century. Even in 2013, in the remoter parts, the nomadic lifestyle subsisted, vignettes of which we could glimpse as we sped through the highlands.

Kirghizia, befitting the appellation 'roof of the world', is home to some of the most stunning mountain ranges of our planet—Alay, Tien Shan and the Pamirs—all of which we crossed at some point during our journey. The Tien Shan range (Heavenly Mountains) extends westward for approximately 370 km from the Chu River and forms part of the border between the two countries.

The next leg of our journey—from Bishkek to Osh, the second largest Kyrgyz city located in the Fergana Valley—took us through the most spectacular landscape of the entire trip. Our delegation transferred to six smaller cars, and we braced ourselves for the very long and bumpy journey ahead. Following some terrorist incidents in the not-too-distant past, buses and vans were not allowed to ply on this route. On these highlands, there was a delicate peace prevailing for the moment, but in 2005, these highlands had seethed with ethnic clashes in which hundreds of people had died.

There were no villages en route, only yurts, and nowhere to stay the night if we got stuck. As we neared the foothills of the Tien Shan range, one of the cars had already sprung a leak and was steadily dripping green coolant all the way, forcing us to make an unscheduled stop to fix the problem. Our Kyrgyz driver was unfazed. He did some jugaad and, voila, we were cruising again through tunnels and mountains, a stunningly beautiful route that needs to be savoured at leisure, not zipped through as we were doing.

The flawless macadam wrapped around the mountains like a giant black serpent. At places, the road plunged into valleys that offered 360-degree horizons with brilliant hues conjured up by an abundance of ozone. The meadows— highland steppes—were draped in emerald. The slopes and valleys were dotted with grazing horses, their silken manes silhouetted against the setting sun. Tribes people in colourful clothes sold solidified mare's milk, a delicacy in these parts. In certain stretches, there were apple orchards; almost all the fruit vendors were women, seated on low stools by the highway with their produce. We kept a watchful eye for the legendary Kyrgyz condor but found only lesser birds of prey.

On the other side of the mountain ranges lie the Fergana cities of Jalalabad and Osh on the Kyrgyz side and historic cities of Uzbek Fergana which includes Andijon from which a mighty Mongol warrior went forth to conquer Bharat and established the Mughal empire. Separated by a quirk of history and caught in political crossfire, the people of the Fergana Valley have learnt to live with uncertainty. On Sulayman hill on the outskirts of Osh was a mazhar and shrine which, the Kyrgyz claimed, were that of Babur, much to the consternation of Uzbeks across the border.

As we rolled into Uzbek Fergana, both sides of the highway had burst into a profusion of blinding white flashes as far as the eye could see. This was cotton country. September was also the fruiting season, and in villages and towns, every home was fronted with trellises, all laden with luscious grapes. Throughout the countryside, there were melons, watermelons, apples, apricots, quinces, persimmons and many other fruits that we did not even recognize. In parks, public spaces, cafes, restaurants and streets, there were fruit trees and the sidewalks were stained with fruit juice. No wonder Babur spoke so nostalgically of the sweetness of the melons of his homeland.

Fergana was just as nostalgic for Zahiruddin Mohammad Babur, its most illustrious son. The legendary Uzbek boy who went on to shape the destiny of Hindustan for the next 300 years seemed to dominate the psyche and public spaces of Fergana. Besides Babur's rather modest home in Andijon, now turned into a museum, there was a Babur Park, a Babur Monument, a Babur International Foundation and several other institutions devoted to the study of Babur's life and times. Fergana was also known for its silk weaving and ceramics, besides other handicrafts.

In our Tashkent hotel, when we came down for breakfast, the dining hall was ringing out with Tamil voices. Surprised, I went to investigate. A brief conversation revealed that the Tamil visitors, merchants and traders from the Tamil heartland, had never heard of Samarkand or Bukhara and could not explain why they were in Uzbekistan in the first place. Curiously, there were no women in the group. Then the penny dropped. Uzbekistan was fast displacing Thailand as the favoured destination of pleasure-seeking men on the prowl.

Samarkand, the next stopover on our itinerary, was indeed the magnet of Central Asia and a prominent town on the ancient Silk Road. I had travelled through Uzbekistan exactly ten years before and visited both Samarkand and Bukhara. Known for its Timurid legacy, Registan, Samarkand's city square, is easily among the most magnificent in the entire world, at par with Emam Square in Isfahan.

Brown-hued and burnished, Bukhara, unlike Samarkand, was a quintessential desert town, an oasis stopover for weary traders embarking upon the punishing wilderness of the Kyzilkum and Karakum deserts, which they must cross to reach the markets in Byzantine. Bukhara's architecture was stark, mostly unglazed and unembellished, emphasizing its rawness and aesthetics. The iconic Kalyan Minaret and Mosque dominate the skyline. Originally built as a beacon to guide travellers, the minaret's unrivalled elegance belies its bloody past. Successive emirs used the top of the minaret to fling convicts down to their death in an age when cruelty was celebrated as the mark of manhood. We wandered through Bukhara's labyrinthine alleys and climbed to the top of the Ark citadel to have a bird's-eye view of this enchanting town.

The very last leg of our journey took us through the Kyzilkum desert, and we had a brief stopover in stunning Khiva, a living museum of Persian and Islamic architecture, once a flourishing slave market and home of Al Khorezmi, the father of algebra. Mohammed ibn Musa al-Khorezmi's systematic approach to solving linear and quadratic equations led to algebra, which has haunted schoolkids all over the world ever since. But his inflictions were not confined only to algebra. He fiddled with the geography of Ptolemy and wrote on mechanical devices such as the astrolabe and the sundial. He assisted in a project to determine the circumference of the earth and in making a world map for Al-Ma'mun, the caliph, overseeing seventy geographers. Al-Khorezmi's statue dominates the square in Ichan Kala, Khiva's nerve centre.

Statue of Mohammed ibn Musa Al-Khorezmi at Khiva

At the Mamun Institute in Khiva—originally set up by Alberuni himself more than 1500 years ago and functioning almost continuously except for a break of about 150 years—there is a museum that gives us a crash course on Uzbek history from the prehistoric times to the present. Al-Khorezmi occupies pride of place in the museum alongside Ibn Sina, the African physician who came to Khiva to heal and cure.

We wrapped up our road trip in Urgench. The journey took us through over 5000 km of the most challenging terrain on earth which now survives only in our memory and a few stills shot by this author. For, our young film-makers missed one minor detail: they forgot to switch on the camera while filming. The trip was particularly memorable for the vast wastelands through which we drove without spotting a human for hours in this otherwise overcrowded planet. The mountains were aloof and lofty; the passes, teetering and dangerous; the river valleys obscenely lush and fecund; the wildernesses, withering and desolate. The cities were redolent of smoky shashlik and iridescent in their gorgeous architecture, the steppes were seemingly never-ending and the desert stretches, unforgiving. Ambitious monuments built by rulers with monumental ambitions dotted the landscape. More than anything else, the trip was valuable for the ringside view it offered of the three Central Asian Republics struggling to break free of the shackles of history and geography to find their rightful place in today's world.

2015

From Ecstasy to Terror in Serengeti

My journey to the savannah actually began in Zanzibar, an island off the coast of East Africa. After a few days in Zanzibar's Stone Town, a UNESCO World Heritage Site, I decide to check out Serengeti, for which the jumping-off point is Kilimanjaro, an hour's flight from Dar es Salaam, the principal city of Tanzania. From school textbooks, we all know that Kilimanjaro is the tallest peak in Africa, but it is only during this journey that I discover how much Mt Kilimanjaro dominates the psyche of Tanzanians. The catamaran that takes us from Zanzibar to Dar es Salaam is named M.V. Kilimanjaro. The taxi that drives me to the airport in Dar es Salaam is sent by Kilimanjaro Cabs. At Dar es Salaam's Julius Nyerere airport, I board an aircraft whose belly is emblazoned with the word Kilimanjaro; on board, I am served Kilimanjaro soft drink and Kilimanjaro toffee and offloaded in, you guessed it, Kilimanjaro airport to a glorious view of Mt Kilimanjaro, resplendent in its lofty snow crown.

My family joins me at Kilimanjaro for a memorable wildlife safari that would bring us face-to-face with the most exotic and prolific wildlife on our planet. Paul Roberts Shayo, our safari organizer, is waiting at the airport to receive us and whisk us off to Moshe, a small town that sits adjacent to four wildlife parks in northern Tanzania: Lake Manyara, Kilimanjaro, Tarangire and Serengeti. The week-long safari will be in a four-wheel drive. Paul packs the vehicle with tents, sleeping bags, lanterns, cooking stuff, groceries, even foldable chairs and tables. Suvale, our cook, sits at the back amidst pots and pans. There are no permanent structures in any of the national parks except for toilets and showers. Travellers take their own equipment and bring it all back meticulously without leaving a trail.

The next day, we drive to Lake Manyara in the hope of seeing the millions of flamingos that flock here to feast on the krill (small crustaceans) in its salty marshes. But the birds are at the other end of the lake and all we can see is a shimmering pink wave. But on this bank, there are other African game galore, especially large groups of hippos, dozens of giraffes, warthogs, zebras and gazelles. Manyara is also home to several herds of African elephants. We watch mesmerized as a huge herd crosses our track, ears flapping like *pankha*s, or fans, in a Mughal court. One by one, they come straight at your vehicle, tower over you, just inches away from your nose, only to make a last-minute turn, deftly avoiding collision. It is a bit unnerving to have wild elephants come so close that you can hear their breathing and count the crinkles and creases on their skin. Unlike their Indian counterparts, females of the species also sport tusks.

The highlight of the trip to Manyara is a lioness with a pair of gambolling cubs. The mother is busy tearing into a buffalo she has just killed while the curious cubs cross the dry riverbed to investigate our vehicle. The anxious mother abandons her kill and comes bounding towards them. With a nudge, she guides them back to their spot under a tree trunk where she can keep an eye on them while feeding on her kill. We move on, reluctantly.

The next day, we head towards the Serengeti National Park. We go through a densely forested and hilly Ngorongoro Conservation Area before entering the park. En route, we make a brief stop at a Masai village. For a fee, the handsome Masai men and women, all decked up in their traditional gear—bright red and blue sarongs and mounds of jewellery made of cowries and horn—come out of their thatched huts and perform a dance. Then they jump one by one to demonstrate their agility, which once used to be judged by their ability to kill a lion with bare hands. We are taken on a round of the village and shown their way of living. Earlier, in Dar es Salaam, I had seen a few Masai tribesmen in traditional dress riding scooters, weaving in and out of the city's horrendous traffic jams.

Tall, ebony-hued, with chiselled features and shaven heads, the Masai are indeed strikingly handsome and their colourful attire sets them apart.

Masai villages used to dot the Serengeti plains, but in the last fifty years, most of them have been moved to the periphery of the national parks. The Masai people are perhaps not the original inhabitants of this land but were itinerant pastoral people who, in recent times, settled down in villages scattered across eastern Africa. The Masai claim they do not hunt wild animals. That they have lived in peace alongside wildlife for generations gives credence to this claim. However, they have learnt to move with the times and make the most of what tourism can do for their economy. The chief of the village we visit speaks impeccable English as he explains Masai customs to visitors. He tells us that they herd cows as much for their blood as for their milk. 'We draw blood from their necks once every few weeks for drinking, but without killing them.' He also tells us how the practice of female circumcision has been discontinued. Malaria and the tsetse fly, which transmits sleeping sickness, are the two factors that limit the Masai population. The Masai have never farmed, a fact in which they take much pride.

The Serengeti safari begins long before you enter the gates of the national park. There is such a profusion of game en route that you wonder where the park begins or ends. Half a dozen giraffes amble alongside your vehicle, making you feel like a character in a *Jurassic Park* movie.

Giant ostriches take a break from their pecking to regard you with curiosity. Their claws are so powerful that with one blow they can crush your vehicle. Playful zebras butt each other and then stand companionably neck to neck as if to let you know they were only bantering. And thousands of wildebeest kick up dust as they cross the road in single file. Seeing so many of them, you are lulled into a sense of complacency. Surely, nothing can be wrong in a planet where so many animals roam freely in the wild.

Our lunch stop is at Naabi Hill, an elevated rocky mound in the heart of Serengeti. It offers unhindered 360-degree views of the horizon. I trudge up to the top to take in the views, dodging dozens of agama lizards. Standing here, it is easy to believe that the earth is one flat burlap-coloured expanse. The black dots we spot yonder are wildebeest.

Serengeti is a money-spinner for Tanzania. Ecotourism employs 6,00,000 local people and brings in $1 billion annually. Yet, Serengeti also cleaves Tanzania and makes the northern half of the country inaccessible. Arusha, the second largest town in Tanzania, nestles at the foot of Mt Kilimanjaro, in the far north of the country. In recent years, a newly discovered gem called tanzanite, similar to blue sapphire, is being mined in Arusha. More expensive than diamond, and marketed aggressively, the tanzanite trade has lent some urgency to the project to connect the north and the south. The soda ash found in Lake Victoria, oil from Uganda, and cotton also have to travel to markets in Dar es Salaam and beyond.

Currently, access to Arusha and Lake Victoria is only possible by air unless you are willing to take a very cumbersome detour. For many years, the Tanzanian government toyed with the idea of building a road through the savannah to link Arusha to the coastal towns in the south. The Serengeti Highway would have run for hundreds of kilometres south to north, but crucially, 53 km of the proposed highway would have cut through the annual migration route. There was much debate within the country and internationally, and eventually, when the government decided to go ahead with the construction of the highway, which should have been completed in 2014, the African Network for Animal Welfare, a non-profit organization, moved the courts and obtained an order against the construction.

We halt at Seronera Camp for the night. There are about a dozen tents. A zinc-sheet-roof cookhouse is a beehive of activity, with a dozen cooks rustling up fresh food for their respective clients. A huge tank provides fresh water, which is brought in daily. Suvale knows how to serve a meal in style, even in this wilderness. He has everything one might think of—fresh fruit, dessert, coffee. After dinner, we gaze at the zillions of stars hanging on a moonless sky. It is an indescribably beautiful night.

And then begins our ordeal. In the middle of the night, we are woken up by the blood-curdling howl of hyenas. There must be dozens of them. We can hear them scampering around our tents, wailing and howling in chorus and at times thrusting their snouts through the thin tent cloth.

Suddenly I feel a tug in my lower abdomen. No, not a hyena, but my own recalcitrant bladder which develops spontaneous incontinence for some reason. The toilet block is some 300 yards away, lit by a single solar lamp. For the rest, there is only starlight. Not only must I brave the howling horde of hyenas, but also skip over dozens of tent ropes to reach my destination. If I trip, the hyenas will have a feast.

Father and son join my hunt for the torch somewhere on the floor of the tent. Finally, we locate it. I unfasten the flap of the tent and gingerly open it. There are more than a dozen pair of glowing eyes watching me, perhaps hoping I am going to throw them some morsels of meat. I panic and shut the flap at once. A few minutes later, they are still there, now silently staring at the tent. By now, my bladder is in no mood to brook any delay. I flash the torch into their eyes and let out a piercing shriek. One backs off a little as I can make out by the two glows moving back. After watching so many programmes on National Geographic and Discovery, I know the trick lies in establishing who is the alpha male in the group. I think I managed it the first time with my scream. I follow it up with another and yet another shriek and steadily advance, flashing the torch all the while.

Gradually, I see several pairs of glowing coals receding farther and farther. Emboldened, I step out of the tent with a pole for additional protection, and make my way to the toilet. It takes all my nerve to cross the 300 yards in full view of the glowing eyes. Eventually, I manage to reach my destination and finish my job. When I return, I find the hyenas have disappeared into the night.

Skydiving at Sixty-Six

As the first rays of the rising sun caress its smooth flanks, Uluru glows red-hot against the surrounding flat scrubland. From this height, it seems every bit as iconic and seductive as the posters make it out to be. But I am unable to appreciate the spectacular views from my uncomfortable position. The body of the plane is just a tiny tin cylinder and I am seated on the floor with my legs stretched out in front of me. There is absolutely no room for manoeuvre. The pilot's cabin is partitioned away just where my foot ends. The roof is inches away from my head and both my palms are resting on the sides of the plane. On the right, the entire side of the tin box makes up the door that had slid up smoothly along the roof to let us—Alois and me—board the plane.

Alois is my tandem guide today. We will be skydiving together. He is sitting uncomfortably close behind me, and his legs are stretched out just outside mine. My head is resting on his chest and I can feel his breath on my cheek. Now you get the drift. Yes, we are literally stacked like two spoons. Alois is busy tethering himself to my life jacket. I can feel the tug of belts going around my belly and back. We boarded as two individuals, but now our destiny is inextricably (I hope) bound together by clasps and straps.

It has been just a few minutes since takeoff and we are already cruising at 15,000 feet and it is time to jump off. Alois slides open the flimsy door to let in a savage gush of wind that almost knocks me out. The roar of the wind makes it impossible for me to even communicate my terror to Alois whom I cannot see.

Alois has recently relocated to Uluru, all the way from his native France. He claims to have successfully completed more than 3000 tandem dives so far, most of them in France. I have my doubts though, considering his youthful face and impish smile.

He nudges me towards the open door where I am supposed to dangle my feet outside the plane, preparatory to the jump. This is the moment of reckoning, the Rubicon I am about to cross. But having signed away my life in an elaborate waiver, indemnifying Uluru Skydiving against any claims by my progeny or by myself if I survive this, I have little choice but to comply. I mutter a silent prayer and fervently hope Alois had not been doing drugs the previous night or nursing a hangover after a heavy boozing session.

I figure it is too late to chicken out now. I heave my legs out of the aircraft, tugging Alois behind me; at once I feel giddy and disoriented. 'Banana, banana!' Alois screams in my ear, hoping to be heard above the din of the merciless wind. Just before we had boarded the plane, Alois had given me a five-minute—mind you, just five-minute— instruction on how to skydive, bending my body like a ripe banana. 'You cross your arms over your chest, arch your back, tilt your head backwards mimicking the shape of a bent banana,' he had told me before we boarded. I had to fill up a form where I had to declare my age as well. 'You're sixty-six? Well, my grandma is younger. I can now persuade her to skydive with me,' he says with a chuckle. And then sagely declares that skydiving has nothing to with one's age, but with one's mental make-up, with all the solemnity that only a twenty-something can muster.

I contort my body into a banana as best I can, considering Alois is strapped to me all the while. The decision to let go—of control over life and limb—is not a conscious one any more. It just happens.

In the next few seconds, I am spinning through the air, hostage to the elements that whirl us round and round rather speedily, like a top. I lose my bearings completely. There is a rush of adrenaline and a sensory overload, a sensation like no other. I have crossed the Rubicon and lost all control over what would happen next. The feeling is more freedom than fear. Nothing matters any more. I feel totally at peace with myself, cobalt-blue skies above seeing me off wistfully, brown earth below rushing towards me like a long-lost lover, the wind caressing my face affectionately and keeping me afloat (apart from the clasp entrusting my destiny to Alois, of course)—the feeling is one of liberation!

At some point, we must have slowed down, whirling around. I catch a fleeting glimpse of the underside of the plane that seems to have shrunk in size and moved away. It is then I realize I have already fallen quite a distance from the moment we dived. I had not felt it because I was whirling away merrily like a top. As I begin to make sense of my bearings, I find myself horizontal, with Alois floating somewhere above me. Alois taps me on my shoulder, asking me to stretch my arms—Kate Winslet style in *Titanic*. Although the earth is speeding towards me at 140 km/hr, I feel I am floating in eternity—an unbearable lightness of being.

Alois taps me again on my shoulder and asks me to look into the GoPro camera strapped to his right hand. My puffer jacket has ballooned to block my face, but he smooths it down for the selfie. How he manages to do this when both of us are hurtling down in free fall still astonishes me. I turn to face the camera and try to smile, but all I can manage is a wan grimace.

Now I begin to notice my surroundings. Yonder, Uluru beckons seductively. Directly below me, the earth seems to be rushing towards us like a spaceship spinning out of control. I can even make out the mounds and shadows and the endless scrubland stretching to the horizon. After about thirty seconds of free fall, Alois yanks the parachute open and suddenly both of us turn vertical with a jerk. From now on, the descent is gradual, allowing me enough time to savour the delights of the outback from this vantage position.

Once taller than the Andes, now reduced to a stub just 348 metres in height, Uluru is nevertheless stunning, whichever angle you view it from. From the sky, it stands out from the rest of the landscape on account of its sheer ochre sheen and shape. From the ground, the chiaroscuro light and shade tantalizes from afar. When you get up close, the mound changes hues dramatically from moment to moment. The striations wrought by elements over millennia on its otherwise smooth surface stand out in stark relief, scored and pitted by dark shadows. These patterns as well as the rest of the outback have inspired thousands of generations of Aboriginal art.

In the twinkling of an eye, we are near the landing point, a brown square of clearing amidst the endless scrubland. A jeep is waiting some distance away. Alois tugs the cord and tells me to get into landing position, which is to lift both my legs up, parallel to the earth. He lands on his feet and pulls down the parachute which is bloated and heavy with the wind. I go careening on my backside and land on Alois's toes. He winces, unstraps himself from me, folds down the recalcitrant parachute and packs it into the jeep. Although I am physically back on Mother Earth, I still feel afloat, light and heady. I wonder why fear was not one of the emotions I felt when jumping out of the aircraft.

Back home, my family refuses to believe I actually skydived at age sixty-six. Thankfully, Alois remembered to send me the GoPro pics. I have even blown up one of these into a poster and stuck it prominently above the dining table to shut them up. But I know I will not skydive again. It is just not thrilling enough.

The author dangling precariously at 12,000 feet manages to feign exhilaration, well almost